GOOD IS THE NEW COOL

GOOD IS THE NEW COOL

MARKET LIKE YOU GIVE A DAMN

AFDHEL AZIZ

&

BOBBY JONES

Regan Arts.

NEW YORK

Regan Arts.
65 Bleecker Street
New York, NY 10012

First Regan Arts hardcover edition, October 2016

Library of Congress Control Number: 2016939710

ISBN 978-1-68245-046-8

Interior and illustration design by Nancy Singer
Cover design by Richard Ljoenes

Images on pages 21, 57, 60, 122, 178, 206, 220 by Freepik.com; page 260 by Vecteezy.com

Printed in the United States of America

10 9 8 7 6 5 4 3 2 1

**FOR OUR
RESPECTIVE SONS,
MILES & NURI**

CONTENTS

INTRODUCTION

WHY WE WROTE

GOOD IS THE NEW COOL

It's a Saturday afternoon in Soho, New York. The streets are packed with shoppers and tourists, all busy exploring the luxury designer stores that are clustered in the area: Paul Smith, Prada, Balenciaga. Yet outside one store is a scene that looks more like a nightclub than a retail outlet, with a velvet rope and security guards. People are lined up outside, patiently waiting their turn, until the crush inside the store reduces enough to let them in. This isn't some high-end luxury boutique; this is a store that sells $95 eyeglasses and for every pair bought, distributes a pair to someone in need. This is Warby Parker.

Inside the store, the lucky ones who have gotten in are eagerly trying on pairs of retro-themed eyewear with names drawn from literature (Beckett, Huxley, Chandler) and Americana (Roosevelt, Marshall, Langston). The look of the store is inspired by the New York Public Library—all rolling ladders and floor-to-ceiling shelves with beautifully presented merchandise and vintage books, all of which helps to convey the inclusive yet aspirational allure of the brand.

Supercool design has been a huge factor in the success of the brand. After all, people want to look good first; regardless of any social good intent, the products themselves have to be appealing. The frames themselves instantly give wearers the kind of bookish, hipster image one sees in the pages of *GQ* and *Vogue* (both of which have covered the brand with the kind of breathless fandom that used to be reserved for Gucci and Tom Ford).

But an equally crucial part of what drives the success of Warby Parker is that for every pair of eyeglasses bought, the equivalent cost is donated to VisionSpring, a nonprofit whose goal is to provide eye care to those in need, both by training people in developing countries to give basic eye exams and by selling affordable glasses.

Instead of a straight donation model, this creates a more sustainable approach, helping build the long-term infrastructure for eye care. To date, more than 2 million pairs of glasses have been distributed across the world. This aspect of Warby Parker is a large part of why wearing the glasses makes devotees of the brand feel so good, and it makes them want to tell others to purchase the brand. In doing so, Warby Parker has managed to create the Holy Grail for brands: a word-of-mouth magnet. A full 50 percent of customers coming to the website do so on the recommendation of a friend.

Warby Parker has managed to come up with something remarkable: a brand that disrupts the status quo economically (selling designer frames for $95), logistically (selling them online), stylistically (taking retro cool to the world), and socially (their impact in the developing world). In doing so, they have also created a business that is now valued at more than $1 billion after just *six years*. How did they do that?

Warby Parker is the perfect example of a brand that has figured out the model for success we unveil in this book: how to "Make Money and Do Good by Harnessing the Power of Cool." They understand that today's customers want it all, and they have created a purpose-driven business all of us can learn from.

But they are far from alone in today's world. Brands like TOMS, Tesla, Etsy, Kickstarter, Patagonia, Ben & Jerry's, and many others are also figuring out how to use this combination of "Commerce, Culture, and Conscience" (as we call it) to create brands with passionately loyal followings. Not to mention the thousands of B Corps (or benefit corporations) out there that have embarked on a mission to upgrade business to go beyond the tired, short-term thinking of only driving shareholder value to the much more profound approach of also driving societal value.

We believe we are witnessing a seismic shift in popular culture—one where doing "Good" has become its own form of "Cool," creating a unique opportunity for brands, nonprofits, and artists to learn from each other and work together. We believe this is being driven by three key factors: the new expectations of millennials and Generation Z, the crisis of meaningfulness in marketing and advertising, and the disruptive opportunities afforded by technology. In the upcoming chapters, we're going to dive deeper into all of these factors and unearth what they mean for us.

Our mission in this book is to track this profound change in the zeitgeist, and also to show you how marketing has a crucial role to play in this brave new world. Marketing is consistently ranked as one of the least valuable professions in society, but we believe this new approach could both elevate it and show how marketing can help save the world. We propose something radical: replacing the broken twentieth century approach to marketing that is fixated on advertising with an altogether new one, where "Great Marketing Optimizes Life."

Seeing this shift in business and culture, we were inspired to learn more about the pioneers that are leading this new movement, and we're going to share our journey with you. We will travel from the boardrooms of Silicon Valley to the mosh pits of alternative music festivals in Brooklyn, from the Cannes Lions advertising festival in France to the streets of Rajasthan, India. We're going to meet men and women from all backgrounds, at all stages of their careers—from the managers of some of the biggest music superstars in the world to the inspiring marketers running brands like Citibank, Zappos and the Honest Company, and some of the hardworking young hustlers and entrepreneurs who are just starting to make a dent in the worlds of business and nonprofits.

We're going to share what we've learned from their journeys in seven principles that can be used by anyone in any organization anywhere. There are lessons on how to "Find Your Purpose" and "Find Your Allies"; how to incorporate principles like "Treat People

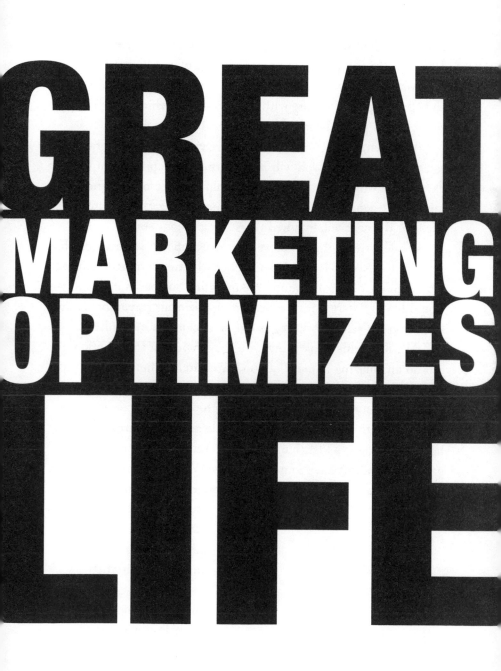

as Citizens Not Consumers" and "Don't Advertise, Solve Problems" as you design and plan; and how to execute ideas of impact by using insights such as "Lead with the Cool," "People Are the New Media," and "Back Up the Promise with the Proof." All which add up to our central idea: "Great Marketing Optimizes Life."

And then, finally, we're going to give you a checklist of how you can take these things you will have learned and apply them to your day-to-day work in a way that will help you personally find more meaning in what you do, and help your organization future-proof itself for the next one hundred years.

While writing this book we had an epiphany: we realized that as marketers, we no longer have to choose between quitting our day job to join a nonprofit (more "meaningful" but perhaps where we would have to start from the beginning again) or staying where we are, doing the same work (respected, well-paid but unfulfilled).

We hope this book shows you that there is a third option: we can do an amazing amount of good from right where we are today, in ways that grow our brands and our businesses, while also contributing to society—a much bigger win-win-win for all.

Because this book is all about people and their purposes, it may help you to know a little bit about us, the authors, and our own purposes. We couldn't have come from two more different backgrounds, but there was something we had in common that drew us to this bigger idea.

BOBBY'S STORY

It was another late night at the office—the time of evening when most parents are tucking their kids into bed, friends are having a round of drinks, or others are maybe just sitting on their couch watching the latest addictive hit show. However, on this evening, like many others before, I was in front of a computer screen staring at a PowerPoint slide and trying to find the perfect image to add to a presentation for a morning meeting. It was December, and my mind was wandering, reflecting on the year that was quickly coming to an end.

We had had a great year—the best year ever—winning big marketing-agency-of-record accounts, helping to transform the way global clients understood youth culture, and becoming award-winning industry leaders in the process.

But as I sat in that office, I was miserable. There were perks to the job, and I worked with great people, but my life was becoming consumed by the stress of the work—seven-day workweeks, constant client demands, internal company revenue pressures, and never-ending fire drills. More and more, I found myself asking questions: *What is all this for? Does this work even matter? Where is the joy in this?* And I wasn't alone. Oftentimes, my clients were just as unhappy and stressed, dealing with all the pressures of selling more things that people were caring less about. I knew there had to be a better way; I just didn't know what it was.

In my heart, I believed I had a bigger purpose than the work I was doing, but I needed help to figure out what it was. After months of procrastination, I finally reached out to the only person I knew who could relate to the position I was in—Tru Pettigrew, my former boss, mentor, and friend. I had witnessed him go through this same stress. I called him one day and simply said I needed help. I was at my wits' end and knew he would understand. What I did not know at the time was that he had recently started his own practice to help others discover their passion and purpose, and he was testing a new model for his work. It was perfect timing! We agreed to start the process the following week, and I began it with a simple prayer: "God, please give me clarity of my purpose and the courage necessary to fulfill it." And with that, we started on a journey of discovery together.

We went through months of exploration to better understand by gifts, passions and purpose. I wrote out my vision for my life, listed the things I valued most, and we talked weekly about my progress and what I was learning from the process; and the final exercise was to put on paper a statement of purpose detailing how I exist to serve. It was a hard exercise, a lot tougher than I would have expected. I struggled for weeks to articulate it and get it right; nothing was more important than gaining the clarity I had previously prayed for. One day in December—a year after that late night in the office—I was traveling to Washington, DC, struggling to write my statement of purpose, and I remembered a story by my friend Eric Dawson. Eric was founder of Peace First, a nonprofit organization I had always admired and for which I had served as a marketing adviser for years. The first time I ever met Eric, he told me a story that had inspired his work:

One evening, an elderly Cherokee brave told his grandson about a battle that goes on inside people. He said, "My son, the battle is between two 'wolves' inside us all. One is evil. It is anger, envy, jealousy, sorrow, regret, greed, arrogance, self-pity, guilt, resentment, inferiority, lies, false pride, superiority, and ego. The other is good. It is joy, peace, love, hope, serenity, humility, kindness, benevolence, empathy, generosity, truth, compassion, and faith."

The grandson thought about it for a minute and then asked his grandfather, "Which wolf wins?"

The old Cherokee simply replied, "The one that you feed."

And it hit me. That is what I've always been trying to do in my work in youth marketing: feed the good wolf. It became crystal clear at that instant that my purpose was to use my gifts and talents to feed the good in young people around the world. That moment of clarity was so powerful it literally gave me chills. Everything that had happened up to that point made so much more sense—it had all happened for a reason.

Unexpectedly, a few weeks later Eric called to catch up. He asked how I was doing, and I told him about my journey and the impact of the story he had shared with me. He could sense the excitement in my voice and the new conflict I was facing of how to fulfill this purpose as a marketer.

He told me he was at a crossroads with Peace First and wanted a partner to help take the work of his small organization and connect it with millions of young people looking to change the world for the better, as peacemakers. He wanted me to be that partner. Some months later I became the chief marketing and communications officer at Peace First, where I am now working to feed the good in millions of young people around the world.

I am sharing my story as a testimony that once you truly seek to influence a greater good, opportunities reveal themselves to do so. My opportunity and journey may be very different from yours, but I wrote this book with Afdhel because I know many of you are working in offices and coffee shops, looking for ways to do more meaningful work, but you just need to know how; and the good news is you don't have to leave your day jobs. My intent is to help fellow marketers use more of their talents and resources to influence a greater good, right where they are.

I hope this book will make a positive impact in the lives of marketers, customers, and our communities while, in the process, helping give me more courage, confidence, and credibility to serve others on a greater scale.

THE TWO
MOST **IMPORTANT** DAYS
OF YOUR LIFE

ARE THE DAY YOU WERE
BORN

and

THE DAY YOU FIND OUT
WHY.

MARK TWAIN

AFDHEL'S STORY

There's a great quote from Mark Twain: "The two most important days of your life are the day you were born, and the day you find out why."

The day I found out why was the day after Christmas in 2004, when the devastating Indian Ocean Tsunami struck the shores of Sri Lanka, my country of birth and where I grew up. I was there for my brother's wedding, but the occasion for joy was overshadowed by one of the biggest natural disasters the country had ever seen. By some miracle, when the wave hit, I was safe in Colombo, the capital city, out of harm's way. More than 30,000 people died on one day, a catastrophe of epic proportions. Like the rest of my friends and family, I got involved in the emergency operations to help the survivors. I can't remember much of the next few weeks; it was a blur of loading up food and medicine trucks, visiting refugee camps, and trying to cope with the sheer immensity of the horror that had struck my beautiful island home.

After the tsunami, I went back to London, where I lived at the time. I would be walking down the street and suddenly burst into tears for no apparent reason. It was only later that I was diagnosed with post-traumatic stress disorder and had to seek counseling. I was diagnosed with survivor guilt: Why had I survived when so many others hadn't? I quit my job and went traveling around the world for six months. I thought a lot about what I wanted to do with my life. I was bone-tired after working around the clock, and I had been chain-smoking two packs a day. And beneath that physical and mental exhaustion, there was something missing: there was no sense of achievement, no sense of joy at what I was doing for a living. I just felt . . . empty. It made me completely reassess what was really meaningful in life and my role in the world.

Up to that point, I had been happy in my chosen career of marketing. But after seeing the death and devastation that had hit the country of my birth, and how little I could do to help it, I started to wonder, did what I do for a living matter in the grand scheme of things? I began to feel that somehow there was something else I could do with my time and energy, something that had a deeper meaning than helping create clever marketing campaigns. I didn't want my legacy on this planet to be that I just helped persuade people to buy more stuff. I wanted to do something more meaningful with the opportunities I had been given in life.

I began to think about ways for marketing to really be innovative. Instead of trying to come up with an even glossier print ad or a more seductive TV spot, what if you could find ways to optimize customers' lives? I wondered if this could be accomplished by creating services, products, and experiences that filled an unmet need in their lives, so that instead of trying to find ways to block marketers out, they would not only appreciate the marketing but also go on to become those marketers' biggest advocates? Was there a way to drive the business and the brand in a way that was also positive for the consumer and society? That was the beginning of the journey that led to collaborating with my friend and coauthor, Bobby.

As authors, our purpose is to inspire others to join in this movement to be better marketers and citizens. In fact, we'd state our goal as simply: "To inspire 100 percent of people reading this book to do 100 percent more good in the world."

And we believe that there is a brand-new model for marketing that allows brands to "Make Money and Do Good by Harnessing the Power of Cool," which we want to explore and unpack in this book.

So let's start by taking a look at the three biggest drivers of this shift in culture that we've observed—generational, technological, and spiritual.

PART I

GOOD IS THE NEW COOL

HOW GOOD BECAME THE NEW COOL

EVERY TIME YOU SPEND MONEY you're casting a VOTE FOR THE TYPE OF WORLD YOU WANT TO LIVE IN.

—Anne Lappe

MILLENNIALS AND GEN Z HAVE NEW EXPECTATIONS OF BRANDS

Looking at the news headlines today, it would be easy to fall into a state of deep despair. Stories of extreme climate change, preventable diseases, economic inequality, social injustice, and the failure of our key institutions—government, banks, and corporations—dominate the news cycles and social media feeds.

Yet from traveling around the world and talking with young people, it is clear the millennial (those born between the early eighties and the mid nineties) and Generation Z (born in the mid nineties) generations have a real sense of optimism about the future of this planet. How can that be?

For many in the media and marketing worlds, millennials have been viewed as the "me" generation. However, for a generation that has proven to be connected and compassionate to the experiences of others around the world, a more appropriate title may be the "we" generation.

Growing up in a time when everything including traditional values, politics, and economics are collapsing and being redefined around them, millennials are experiencing a unique confluence of empathy and empowerment. Connected via myriad social media platforms and mobile devices,, this generation has been able to see and share experiences of troubles and unrest in real time, creating a "glocal" sense of shared struggle with their peers around the world.

There is also a collective feeling by young people that these adverse conditions were created by a previous generation of adults who screwed it up for everyone. However, these young people are not playing the role of the victim; rather, they are seizing the opportunity to do something about it—to help make things better, while along the way redefining societal norms and disrupting business as usual.

Younger generations want experiences over products, sharing versus sole ownership, and entrepreneurship versus employment. And these shifts in values are for good reason: these younger generations have seen their parents' generation work themselves to the bone to— quoting finance expert Dave Ramsey—"Buy things they don't need, with money they didn't have to impress people they didn't like," only to see them lose it all to financial crises and downsizing.[1]

Consider these statistics: Millennials in the United States number 80 million and have a combined annual spending power of $200 billion (and a staggering $2.45 trillion globally). And according to the 2015 Cone Communications Millennial CSR Study 91 percent would switch brands to one associated with a cause (versus the US average of 85 percent). In addition, the report states this group is also more likely to purchase a product with a social or environmental benefit, and volunteer for a cause supported by a company they trust.[2]

The situation is no different when we look at the generation hot on the heels of millennials: Generation Z. Numbering 80 million, Generation Z has a direct spend of $44 billion, which rises to $200 billion when you consider the indirect influence they have over their parents' spend. And according to the Fuse Gen Z Report on Social Activism and Cause Marketing after learning a brand supports a social cause, 85 percent are likely to purchase from that brand over another brand that does not support a cause (vs. 70 percent of millennials who do so).[3]

Both of these generations have realized, to quote the writer Anna Lappé, "Every time you spend money, you're casting a vote for the type of world [you] want to live in."

---

1 Dave Ramsey, *The Total Money Makeover: A Proven Plan for Financial Fitness.* (Nashville: Thomas Nelson Pub., 2009).

2 Cone Communications. "Millennial CSR Study." September 23, 2015. http://www.conecomm.com/2015-cone-communications-millennial-csr-study-pdf.

3 "Future Consumer's Views Social Activism & Cause Marketing." Fuse Marketing. 2015. http://www.fusemarketing.com/future-consumers-views-social-activism-cause-marketing-differs-millennials-think.

But these trends don't just affect purchase decisions; for CEOs and business leaders, they have a profound impact around hiring and retaining the right talent. And according to the PWC "Millennials at Work: Reshaping the Workforce" report, by the year 2025, millennials will fuel approximately 75 percent of the US workforce and 50 percent of the worldwide workforce.[4]

Increasingly, millennials want to work for companies that have a higher purpose than just making profit—the kind of ethical, stakeholder-driven companies that think about people and the planet, not just profit. According to Deloitte's 2015 Millennial Survey, a staggering 84 percent of millennials say making a positive difference in the world is more important than professional recognition. And six out of ten millennials said a sense of purpose (more than just making a profit) is part of the reason they chose to work for their current employer.[5]

In other words, the social currency of creating things that make a positive impact in the world has replaced the cachet of owning things that don't. These younger generations have taken to heart the words of P. Diddy, who, in the movie *Notorious*, says to Biggie, "Don't chase the paper, chase the dream."

This belief is now being echoed by such visionary CEOs as Unilever's Paul Polman, who sees the need for purpose as a crucial part of dealing with the existential crisis facing many companies. Polman told the *Washington Post* in 2015, "You see how many companies are searching for purpose, and how many have a short existence. The average length of a U.S. company is now 18 years. The average length

---

4 "Millennials at Work: Reshaping the Workforce." PriceWaterhouseCooper. https://www.pwc.com/m1/en/services/consulting/documents/millennials-at-work.pdf.

5 "Mind the Gaps: The 2015 Deloitte Millennial Survey." DTTL, 2015. http://www2.deloitte.com/content/dam/Deloitte/global/Documents/About-Deloitte/gx-wef-2015-millennial-survey-executivesummary.pdf.

of a CEO is less than four years. It's not just about making money, especially for the millennial generation. They want to make a difference in life, so they look for companies that have a strong purpose."[6]

And the situation is the same when looking at Gen Z as employees and entrepreneurs: According to a 2014 Intern Sushi/CAA survey, 60 percent want to have an impact on the world with their jobs, compared to 39 percent of millennials.[7]

Thus it is clear that building purpose-driven companies and brands that practice purpose-driven marketing is not only crucial for survival today but for ensuring you "future-proof" yourself for the next two generations of customers and talent.

6 Cunningham, Lillian. "The Tao of Paul Polman." *WashingtonPost*, May 21, 2015. https://www.washingtonpost.com/news/on-leadership/wp/2015/05/21/the-tao-of-paul-polman/.

7 Wartzman, Rick. "Coming Soon to Your Office: Gen Z." *Time*, February 12,2014. http://time.com/6693/coming-soon-to-your-office-gen-z/.

Don't *chase*
THE PAPER
CHASE
the
DREAM

—from the movie *Notorious*

THE DISRUPTIVE IMPACT OF TECHNOLOGY ON ADVERTISING

For years, the advertising model was based on finding out what consumers were paying attention to and creating ways to interrupt those experiences with a brand message. But people didn't want to be interrupted, especially with messages that weren't adding any value to their lives. So over the past two decades, smart innovators, frustrated with the intrusive nature of advertising, have given consumers the ability to control those interruptions, putting the power back in the hands of the people and creating a huge headache for traditional marketers.

At first DVRs allowed you to skip past ads on TV; now we have a new generation who are "cutting the cord" altogether and dispensing with conventional cable TV. According to a Pew Research Center survey, 19 percent of adults between the ages of eighteen and twenty-nine have become cord cutters, dropping cable or satellite TV service, while another 16 percent have never had a traditional subscription TV package.[1] Today it is possible to buy an Apple TV and subscribe to new ad-free models like Netflix, HBO GO, and Hulu—which means there is now a way never to have to see an ad on a TV screen ever again.

Moving from TV to digital the situation doesn't get any better. Ad-blocking software that allows people to block ads on their computer or mobile browsers has been installed by an astonishing 200 million people globally. In fact, ad blocking is estimated to cost publishers an estimated $27 billion in lost revenue by 2020.[2] As

---

1 "Home Broadband, 2015," Pew Research Center, Washington, D.C. (December 21, 2015). http://www.pewinternet.org/2015/12/21/home-broadband-2015/.

2 Barker, Sam. "Worldwide Digital Advertising: 2016–2020." Juniper Research, 2016. http://www.juniperresearch.com/press/press-releases/ad-blocking-to-cost-publishers-$27bn-in-lost-reven.

marketers, we have only ourselves to blame; we continued to bombard people with banner ads and pop-ups, and technology provided them with a way to fight back.

Here's our prediction: Technology is going to do to the advertising business what it did to the music business. The impact of the shift to digital in music was catastrophic for many of the established labels, and it will happen again—this time with the major advertising agencies playing the part of the record labels. Mobile ad-blocking software available in the Apple Store? That's the equivalent of Napster arriving on the scene. It represents a seismic shift of power into the hands of consumers, allowing them to completely control their experience. In the case of the music business, it led to consumers being able to access any music any time anywhere on any device, ending the stranglehold the record labels had over them. In the case of the ad business, it's going to lead to customers blocking out annoying commercials and choosing *exactly* what content they want to interact with.

To compound matters, all the industry has done is try to mask ads and deliver them in other forms. For instance, "native" advertising—which mimics editorial news articles—is the hot topic as this book is being written. In a survey done by Contently, 48 percent of respondents have felt deceived upon realizing a piece of content was sponsored by a brand and 62 percent of respondents think a news site loses credibility when it publishes native ads.[3]

According to McKinsey's Global Media Report, total global media spending will rise from US $1.6 trillion in 2014 to a projected US $2.1

---

3 Joe Lazauskus, "Study: Article or Ad? When It Comes to Native, No One Knows." Contently.com, September 8, 2015. https://contently.com/strategist/2015/09/08/article-or-ad-when-it-comes-to-native-no-one-knows/.

trillion in 2019.[4] But with these generational and technological trends, conventional advertising and media is in danger of becoming irrelevant in the next few decades. Wouldn't it be amazing if we could find new models to channel that investment to marketing platforms that have a more positive and enduring effect? We believe we are at a crossroads: we can either choose to try to prop up an old model that is broken, or we can create a new model that is fit for the unique challenges we see today.

4 Moinak Bagchi, Sonja Murdoch, and Jay Scanlan. "The State of Global Media Spending." McKinsey & Company. December 2015. http://www.mckinsey.com/industries/media-and-entertainment/our-insights/the-state-of-global-media-spending.

THE CRISIS OF MEANING- FULNESS IN MARKETING

I n addition to the massive generational and technological shifts, in the course of writing this book, we realized there is a fundamental spiritual shift happening within the marketing community.

Although businesses have made many meaningful contributions to the betterment of our world, it is also well-documented that corporations have been responsible for all sorts of crimes against humanity, ranging from massive environmental damage and pollution to predatory mortgages to sweatshop labor.

Furthermore, while marketing has also been responsible for building brands and driving businesses that give millions of people jobs, many campaigns created by marketers have actually harmed humanity. Joe Camel and the Marlboro Man inspired generations of young people to start smoking, while Photoshopped imagery that created unrealistic and unattainable appearance goals caused body-image issues for generations of young girls. Marketers have helped to create a culture of materialistic excess that has led to the cancer of overconsumption. And even today marketers are all too often guilty of "greenwashing" or "brandwashing"—marketing their brands and corporations as paragons of virtue while ignoring insidious practices and reprehensible behavior behind the scenes.

That is why it's no surprise that according to Morten Albaek, CEO of Voluntas Investment and former CMO of the Danish company Vestas, "The fact of the matter is that consumers don't trust marketing. Advertisers regularly poll as the least trustworthy professionals, scraping the bottom alongside politicians and civil servants. Can we as individuals accept that these odds are no longer

THE FACT OF THE MATTER IS THAT CONSUMERS DON'T TRUST MARKETING

tactics

strategy

wants

goals

plan

product

sales

method

MORTON ALBAEK

promotion

target

tenable, that we have a moral responsibility to redress such inequities in the modern marketplace?"[1]

We have reached a tipping point where the majority of the world hates what we do. In survey after survey, marketing is listed as one of the least valuable professions to humanity. A 2012 survey carried out by Adobe showed that 68 percent of people found advertising to be "annoying and distracting," with 53 percent reporting "most marketing is a bunch of bullshit."[2]

That same survey listed advertising/marketing as being amongst the bottom four most valuable professions to humanity (the top four being teacher, scientist, engineer, and social worker). What was most surprising was that the survey included people in the advertising/marketing profession—who were *more than twice as likely* as the average person to rank their profession as useless! It signals a deep "crisis of meaningfulness" in what we do for a living.

The desire to find more meaning in what we did for a living was the catalyst for us to start writing this book. And we realized we were not alone: in private conversations with our peers, many told us they were feeling professionally unfulfilled. As dreamers and doers who give brands voices, personalities, and power, they were rewarded well to use their talents to optimize profits, but they were increasingly inspired to optimize people's lives. We were all internally struggling with how to maintain a balance between being good marketers and being good citizens.

Formerly a partner and chief creative officer at Crispin Porter +

---

1 Deborah Malone, "Trendsetters: Vestas' Morten Albaek Urges CMOs to Take a 'Transparency Pledge' at The Internationalist 100 Event." *Internationalist Magazine.com*, May 13, 2012. http://internationalistmagazine.com/Trendsetter/Trendsetter_2012_may13_more.html.

2 "Click Here: The State of Online Advertising." October 2012. http://www.adobe.com/aboutadobe/pressroom/pdfs/Adobe_State_of-Online_Advertising_Study.pdf.

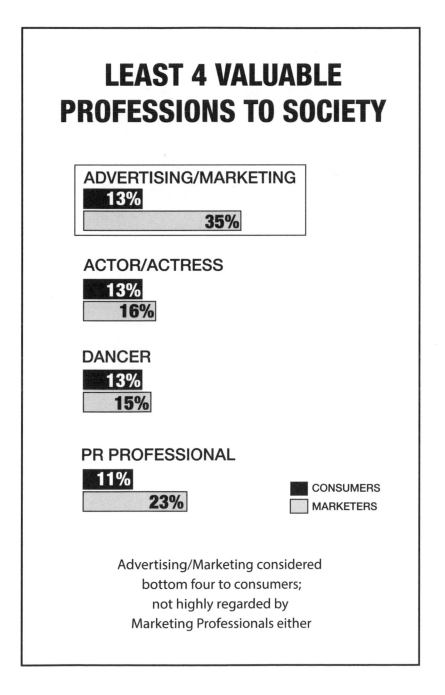

Bogusky, Jeff Benjamin is one of the most respected creatives in the advertising business. He had an epiphany one day he told us about: "I was watching the movie *Deep Impact*, about an asteroid hitting the Earth. In the movie, they create a shelter inside a mountain to safeguard the best of humanity—doctors, engineers, scientists. I was watching the movie, and it hit me . . . what I do for a living wouldn't help me make it into the mountain."

That's a great way to frame this problem: How do we do work that helps us make it into the mountain?

THE
NEW
MODEL
OF
MARKETING

THE
TIME
IS NOW

Here's the good news: the idea that business has enormous potential to be a force for good is moving from niche to mainstream. Harvard Business School professor Michael Porter summarized the huge opportunity of the situation in a TED Talk titled "Why Business Can Be Good at Solving Social Problems." The following chart shows that by an order of magnitude, resources are concentrated in the hands of corporations.

This recognition of the power of corporations to drive positive social impact at scale is redefining the expectations of how corporations should behave.

TNT Express CEO Tex Gunning summed it up perfectly when he said in an interview in *EnlightenNext* magazine, "Average leaders take care of themselves and their families. Good leaders take care of themselves, their families, and some of the community. Great leaders—and great companies—not only take care of these stakeholders but also want to change the world. They want to leave the world better than they found it."[1]

In fact, we believe we are seeing a new evolution of capitalism—Conscious Capitalism—when customers, more than ever before, are demanding the brands and corporations in their lives demonstrate a positive effect on social issues. And to us the inference is simple: we believe Conscious Capitalism requires Conscious Marketing.

We believe the time is right for marketers to accept the challenge to lead organizations toward being forces for greater good. We believe marketers are exactly the kind of thoughtful, resourceful, versatile, inspirational people who are needed right now to address those inequities. We understand how to speak the languages of

---

1 "I Have No Choice." Interview with Tex Gunning by Elizabeth Deblod. *EnlightenNext.*/Vol. 28, March–May 2005.

NONPROFITS
$1.2 trillion

GOVERNMENT
$3.1 trillion

WHERE ARE THE RESOURCES?

Total revenue by stakeholder,
United States

CORPORATIONS
$20.1 trillion

Source: Michael Porter TED.com

finance, R&D, sales, and marketing. We have the ability to speak to customers, understand what they need, spot market opportunities, and create propositions, products, and strategies for launching them into the world. We partner with designers, technologists, and artists to create conversations. We are well positioned to be the change makers in our organizations. In short, it is time for us to "Market Like We Give a Damn."

Marketers are the ones in an organization who are the champions of the customer. Practicing marketing like you actually give a damn about the lives of your customers means seeing what really matters to them. Nine times out of ten, it won't be another piece of advertising; it will be something that helps them optimize their lives. In other words, we're saying not to use the tools of your trade to find ways to emotionally manipulate people; instead find ways to use the tools to inspire them, encourage them, and help them.

And in the process, we want to market like we give a damn about the wider impact marketing has on our neighborhoods and cities, on the environment and ecosystem. As the human population grows from 7 to 8 billion, and more and more people buy consumer products, the decisions we make as marketers—on product, on supply chain, on where marketing investments should flow—will have a profound impact. It is up to us to think in terms of marketing that delivers a triple bottom line in terms of profit, yes, but also in terms of people and planet.

To put it more bluntly: If we don't deal with income inequality, no one is going to be able to afford our products. If we don't deal with climate change, there's not going to be anybody left to buy them.

We think that in addition to the classical four P's of marketing (product, price, place, and promotion) there is now a fifth P: "purpose." People want the brands they support to stand for more than profit, and they want to see that purpose brought to life in clear and tangible ways that benefit society and the planet. Today marketers have the responsibility to find ways to create "purpose-driven marketing"—and lead a team that not only includes their corporate social responsibility (CSR) counterparts but also CTOs, CFOs, and other leaders from every single part of the organization to radically rethink the ways in which their brands can do well by doing good. It is a golden opportunity to elevate marketing from being a profession that is hated to one that is admired.

But this new attitude needs a new model to make it work. The consumer expectation that brands do more good, coupled with the cool factor good now has, allows for smart marketers to develop big ideas that are cool, do good, and make money. This is creating disruption and opportunities not only in the way products are marketed but also in how they are developed, designed, and sold.

In our journey for this book, we met an inspiring new generation of marketers, social entrepreneurs, and culture creators who are out to change our world for the better. Sharing a collective sense of responsibility to help address the environmental, civic, and economic ills that are affecting all of us, these visionaries aspire not just to help change market conditions but also human conditions.

We were able to distill what they have learned into a model we think could replace the broken, traditional marketing model with something fresher and more meaningful.

HOW TO HARNESS THE POWER OF COOL

Building on our belief "Great Marketing Should Optimize Life," we think that today there is a powerful new model where brands ("Commerce"), nonprofits ("Conscience"), and artists ("Culture") can work together to "Make Money and Do Good by Harnessing the Power of Cool."

Each of these entities has valuable strengths. Brands with their budgets and customer bases have reach and resources; nonprofits have in-depth knowledge of how to solve issues and armies of workers and volunteers dedicated to their cause; and artists have the ability to shine a spotlight on an issue, and help engage their fan bases.

Working together allows us to solve issues within each of our own industries. Brands that genuinely find purpose and align themselves with nonprofits and artists to create large-scale, meaningful ways to solve people's problems, will be able to solve the "trust gap" with consumers and turn them into their biggest advocates. Artists who partner with brands and nonprofits in sustainable and respectful ways can use their talents to not only give them new canvases, but also leave behind a moral legacy as well as an artistic one. And social entrepreneurs who create alliances of integrity with the right artists and brands can find ways to use the power of cool to do more good than if they tried on their own.

We all need each other to make what we do more meaningful, more powerful, and reach more people. To do that, we should follow these seven principles.

1. Know Your Purpose: The greatest companies today have a higher-order purpose than just profit. Disney's is "We create happiness by providing the finest in entertainment for people of all ages,

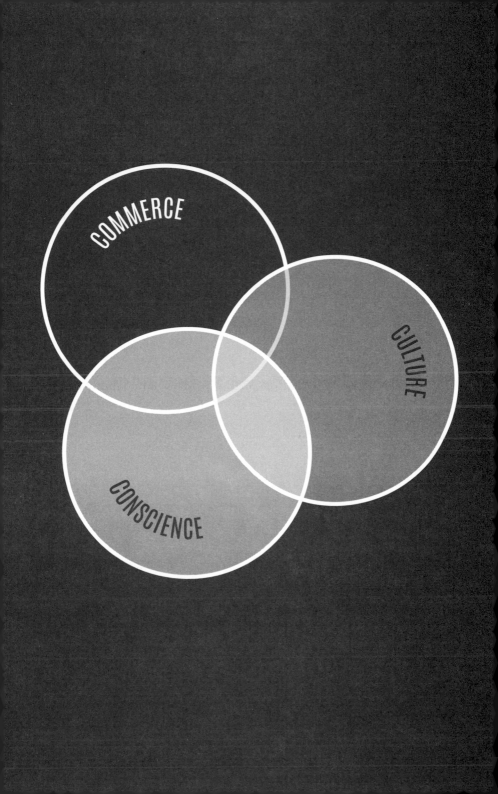

everywhere," Tesla's is "To accelerate the world's transition to sustainable energy," and Nike's is "To bring inspiration and innovation to every athlete in the world." Think about how inspiring these purposes are to the customers and employees of these companies—far more than any quarterly profit goal. Finding your brand's higher-order purpose is the first step to unlocking a tremendous amount of meaning and potential.

2. Find Your Allies: Today's brands must build coalitions of allies with common purpose—especially with nonprofits (who bring an in-depth knowledge of how to solve issues) and "Architects of Cool" (who are able to shine a cultural spotlight and ignite societal change). That's a terrifically powerful way to tackle the massive problems facing the world today. As the African proverb says, "If you want to go fast, go alone. If you want to go far, go together."

3. Think Citizens, Not Consumers: We believe that if you only treat people as "consumers" of your product, you are condemned to have only a one-dimensional relationship with them. Conversely, if you treat people as "citizens"—with a range of passions, concerns, and goals—you will be able to have a much richer, multidimensional relationship with them. In that relationship your purpose as a brand can find common ground with their purpose; instead of being in a "transactional" relationship, you can be in a "transformational" relationship.

4. Lead with the Cool: Today it is no longer just enough for a brand to be "good"; it must also be "cool." It must have great design and a great story, and it must be an object of desire. People don't buy Warby Parker glasses just because buying a pair donates another pair to a person in need. They buy them because they have amazing designs at great prices, conveniently available online or in great store experiences. Smart, socially impactful brands from Method to Tesla know the "power of cool" in helping shift behavior.

5. Don't Advertise, Solve Problems: Instead of just defaulting to advertising as the solution to everything, we believe the natural intersection that brands can and should focus on is adding value to their consumers' lives by solving problems. These problems could range from the "everyday" (e.g., time-saving services and products) to the "epic" (e.g., ending poverty, income inequality, or environmental pollution). What brands choose to work on depends on their organizational purpose and goals.

6. People Are the New Media: In an age of increasing ad blocking, how do you communicate your message at scale? According to a study by Nielsen, 92 percent of people trust recommendations from friends and family more than all other forms of marketing.[1] And 81 percent of US online customers' purchase decisions are influenced by their friends' social media posts.[2] Marketers should be obsessive about creating marketing experiences, products, and services that are so good people will want to spontaneously tell their friends, coworkers, and family about them.

7. Back Up the Promise with the Proof: "Young people have been marketed to since they were babies, they develop this incredibly sophisticated bullshit detector, and the only way to circumvent the bullshit detector is to not bullshit," says Vice founder Shane Smith.[3]

---

1 "Global Trust in Advertising and Brand Messages Report." Nielsen, 2012. http://www.nielsen.com/us/en/insights/reports/2012/global-trust-in-advertising-and-brand-messages.html.

2 Rebecca Scanlan, GroundFloor Media. "Market Force Study Shows Companies Wield Comparable Social Media Influence to Friends." News release, May 1, 2012. Prweb.com. http://www.prweb.com/releases/socialmedia/retail/prweb9456629.htm.

3 Shane Smith, "Vice's Shane Smith: 'Young people are angry and leaving TV in droves.'" Interview by Jon Swaine. TheGuardian.com, March 2, 2014. https://www.theguardian.com/media/2014/mar/02/vice-media-shane-smith-north-korea.

THE "GOOD IS THE NEW COOL" MODEL
GREAT MARKETING OPTIMIZES LIFE

1 KNOW YOUR PURPOSE

2 FIND YOUR ALLIES

3 THINK CITIZENS, NOT CONSUMERS

4 LEAD WITH THE COOL

5 DON'T ADVERTISE, SOLVE PROBLEMS

6 PEOPLE ARE THE NEW MEDIA

7 BACK UP THE PROMISE WITH THE PROOF

HOW TO MAKE MONEY AND DO GOOD
BY HARNESSING THE
POWER OF COOL

Make sure you back up the "Promise" of the brand (your marketing communication) with the "Proof" (actual tangible evidence of the good you are doing). Otherwise your customers and community will expose it for the empty rhetoric it is.

TO SUMMARIZE OUR POINT OF VIEW: instead of creating yet more advertising, your goal should be to create "purpose-based" marketing experiences and services that are so inspirational, educational, or useful that they create an army of advocates to help spread the story of your brand in a rich, authentic way. That's how we think "Great Marketing Optimizes Life," and that's how marketers can find more meaningfulness in the work they do.

In the next couple chapters, we're going to cover the greatest allies brands have: the Architects of Cool and the New Nonprofits. When they all work together, they create an amazing opportunity to "Make Money and Do Good by Harnessing the Power of Cool."

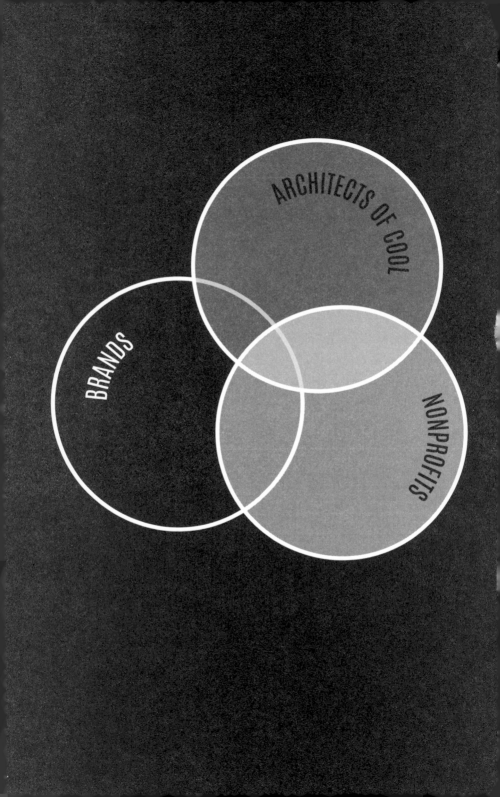

THE ARCHITECTS OF COOL ARE ON YOUR SIDE

Here's some more good news for brands: the Architects of Cool are on your side.

Who are the Architects of Cool? We classify them as cultural entrepreneurs, storytellers, and artists (whether in the fields of music, film, visual art, or others), designers (in the fields of fashion, products, and architecture), and others (athletes, journalists). They are the people who drive culture forward, who help shape the popular agenda, who define the indefinable "cool." Beyond being simply the engine of entertainment, there is a growing realization that cool should also be a force for good. We see these Architects of Cool increasingly using their fame, reach, and resources to drive global awareness and change across areas such as public health, youth advocacy, and education. As Lady Gaga says, "I don't want to make money; I want to make a difference."[1] And the Architects of Cool can become some of your greatest allies in this new model.

Many of today's leading culture creators have realized they can and should contribute something that is more tangible than another record or movie—from Russell Simmons's work to inspire health and happiness to Arcade Fire's work with Partners in Health in Haiti or Linkin Park's Music for Relief, which focuses on natural disasters. As Simmons himself noted, "There is nothing good about fame unless it inspires happiness in others."[2]

Using "Cool" to do "Good" has a long history, whether you look at the Concert for Bangladesh organized by Ravi Shankar and Beatle George Harrison or the legendary Live Aid concerts of the 1980s. But beyond these models, the Architects of Cool have found all-new ways

---

1 "Lady Gaga: The Interview." Interview with Lady Gaga by Derek Blasberg. HarpersBazaar.com, April 13, 2011. http://www.harpersbazaar.com/celebrity/latest/news/a713/lady-gaga-interview/.

2 Russell Simmons, Twitter Post. August 17, 2013, 7:28 PM. https://twitter.com/unclerush/status/368876916570193920.

I DON'T WANT TO MAKE

MONEY

I WANT TO MAKE A

Difference

Lady Gaga

to leverage their fame for positive social impact. Later in the book we'll look at Bono's Product (RED), an artist-created social-good platform that allowed myriad brands, such as Apple, Nike, Starbucks, and the Gap to get involved in the fight against HIV/AIDS.

In fact, for the Architects of Cool looking to create social impact at scale, brands with their financial resources and huge reach have become their partners of choice. Later in the book, we'll explore how Lady Gaga's Born This Way Foundation has partnered with brands ranging from Mattel to Viacom, and dive into fashion designer Alexander Wang's collaboration with the nonprofit DoSomething.

The Architects of Cool include designers who are making beautiful, desirable products that also have a net social good. Designers such as Apple's Jonathan Ive and Yves Béhar have helped put design at the forefront of popular culture. Béhar in particular has been a vocal proponent of this idea, stating, "Design needs a new relationship with the world, one that is more focused on our planet's needs."[3]

From packaging and interfaces to architecture and wearable technology, designers are applying the lessons from William McDonough's Cradle to Cradle movement, which posits that good design isn't just about surface aesthetics, it's also about having a deep understanding of how and where your products are made and what their long-term impact on the planet will be. Later in the book, we'll talk to Marco Vega from the small agency We Believers, which has been making big waves recently with its creation of edible six-pack rings for beer companies (the rings become food for aquatic life), helping reduce the amount of harmful plastic waste in the ocean.

Whether it's Lady Gaga or a sneaker designer sitting down to her first day of work at Nike, these Architects of Cool now increasingly have a new mission—how to use their power of "Cool" to do "Good."

---

3 Nicole Perlroth, "Yves Behar: The World's 7 Most Powerful People in Design." *Forbes.com*, November 2, 2011. http://www.forbes.com/sites/nicoleperlroth/2011/11/02/yves-behar-the-worlds-7-most-powerful-designers/#7cf2e67b7762.

THERE IS NOTHING GOOD ABOUT

FAME

UNLESS IT INSPIRES OTHERS

RUSSELL SIMMONS

DESIGN needs a new relationship with the world,

Yves Behar

one that is more focused on our planet's **NEEDS.**

THE NEW NONPROFITS

n addition to the Architects of Cool, there is another extremely important set of players that brands should consider partnering with—the nonprofits of the world. Historically, brands have either seen nonprofits only as recipients of corporate largesse—receiving donations from corporate social responsibility programs—or as a partner to carry out some sort of "cause-marketing" initiative. This is not to denigrate those CSR or cause-marketing programs but is instead to encourage brands to go beyond these traditional models and see nonprofits as partners that can bring a unique set of complementary skills to the task of "making money and doing good."

What excites us is a new wave of nonprofits being run by a new generation of leaders who are open to building coalitions and alliances between brands and artists that have never been seen before. Perhaps the biggest difference is their unwillingness to see the world in traditional terms. Take, for instance, Adam Braun, the CEO of Pencils of Promise, one of the most audacious and entrepreneurial start-ups to emerge in recent years. Adam's journey began with a child begging in the streets of India asking him for a pencil. This simple exchange inspired him to create a nonprofit that has achieved an amazing amount of success in a short time.

Adam's enlightened world-view is also bolstered by the techniques he brought with him after years of working in the finance and management-consultancy industries. Adam and his team run Pencils of Promise with a level of accountability and efficiency that would shame many for-profit businesses. The success of this approach can be seen in the fact that at the time this book is going to press, not only can Pencils of Promise claim to have built 342 schools—serving 33,883 students since 2009—they are also breaking ground on new schools at the frankly astonishing rate of one every ninety hours.

This results-driven, transparent approach has also brought on corporate partners ranging from fashion brands like Warby Parker, Dolce & Gabbana, and Versace to media brands like AOL, Vogue, and Google. And thanks to Adam's brother Scooter Braun (whom we interview later in the book), who manages a certain Mr. Justin Bieber, Pencils of Promise has also gained a huge amount of publicity and traction amongst a younger audience, through Justin's support and advocacy of the program.

Another great example of a nonprofit that takes a fresh and radical approach is "charity: water," started by former nightclub entrepreneur Scott Harrison. After a decade of debauchery in the New York club scene, Scott had an epiphany one New Year's Day that led him to start volunteering as a photojournalist on the Mercy Ships, a floating hospital serving the people of Liberia. What he saw on that trip profoundly changed him. He came back and was inspired to throw a birthday party celebration where his guests were invited to donate money to clean water wells in Africa. The response was so great it led him to found charity: water, which to date has created more than 20,000 clean-water projects in twenty-four countries, raising more than $65 million dollars from 300,000 passionate and engaged donors. The projects have prevented more than 5.2 million people from having to walk miles to get water from unsafe sources, saving them time and improving their health in exponential ways.

Scott runs the organization more like a start-up than a traditional nonprofit. Log onto charity: water's website and you see design and branding that would be the envy of many brands. The design is clean and consistent, and well-thought-out assets—from press kits to campaign materials to videos—are easily downloadable and shareable. This sophisticated brand-led approach has also brought on board sponsors like American Express, Caterpillar, and Nautica.

A great example of a nonprofit that has mastered how to "Harness the Power of Cool" is Global Citizen, which was started by Hugh Evans, a young man from Australia, with the inspiring goal of ending the extreme poverty of 1.2 billion people (around 20 percent of the world's population). At the age of fourteen, he returned from a visit to a slum in Manila and announced to his mother that he wanted to dedicate his life to ending extreme poverty.

Hugh's strategy has involved staging large-scale music festivals on the Great Lawn of Central Park: the 2016 edition included music from Rihanna, Kendrick Lamar, Metallica, and Major Lazer and corporate partners like Gucci Chime for Change, Johnson and Johnson, and Live Nation. You may think this sounds like a pretty traditional approach, similar to Live 8, in that it acted as a catalyst for world leaders meeting at the UN to commit to financial and legislative packages to help end extreme poverty. But the added twist was that you couldn't buy a ticket to the concert—you could only earn one by performing a range of actions, from watching and sharing videos about a topic to donating money to charities like UNICEF and Rotary International.

In summary: Nonprofits have in-depth knowledge of a particular problem and how to solve it; they have experts and resources in the places that need them the most. Nonprofits have communities that have a deep sense of purpose and belief in their missions, that are willing to go to extreme lengths and make great sacrifices to help others. As brands become more useful and start to tackle some of the biggest problems of humanity—climate change, poverty, equality for all—they would be foolish to discount nonprofits as key partners that can complement their scale, reach, and resources.

PART II

THE SEVEN PRINCIPLES OF HOW TO MARKET LIKE YOU GIVE A DAMN

1.
KNOW
YOUR
PURPOSE

We start with what is probably the most important principle: Know Your Purpose. Whether it's your personal purpose in life or your organization's purpose, it's important to be clear about what it is—and how it can be of service to others. True purpose is always in service to something bigger than yourself.

One of the most inspiring entrepreneurs of our times, Elon Musk—the founder of hugely purpose-driven companies Tesla, SpaceX, and SolarCity, among others—puts it another way: "Putting in long hours for a corporation is hard. Putting in long hours for a cause is easy."

In this section, we discover how entrepreneur Scooter Braun finds common purpose in all the work he does—whether for his artists, the people who work for him, or the philanthropic work he does. Aria Finger, the CEO of DoSomething.org, shares how she finds purpose in serving a community of 5.2 million young people around the world to help make a change. And we meet millennial founder Matthew Clough, whose inspiring for-profit company Stone & Cloth is creating amazing bags that help fund children's education in Africa.

Scooter Braun

Founder, SB Projects

How did "purpose" go from the subject of academic journals and TED talks to something that is now part of pop culture? Well, some of the credit must lie with Scooter Braun, who first discovered Justin Bieber as a twelve-year-old singing on YouTube. After signing him to his management company, he steered Justin from his early days through his infamous rocky adolescence back to his current-day dominance of the charts. Braun and Bieber have partnered on one of the greatest redemption stories in pop music, though at the heart of this wasn't some calculated strategy but a genuine journey of finding true purpose. Using the power of music, Scooter has been able to open up the idea of purpose to a whole new generation of young people.

It's a packed concert amphitheater in Seattle, and the biggest pop star in the world, Justin Bieber, is standing onstage in front of a white grand piano and a crowd of 16,000 fans. It's the opening night of his world tour and he is speaking from the heart about how he lost his purpose and found it again, before launching into the song "Purpose," from his hit album of the same name. The crowd goes wild, singing along to every line.

Named one of *Time* magazine's 100 Most Influential People, Scooter Braun has diversified his portfolio via his company, SB Projects, which not only manages talent like Kanye West, Black Eyed Peas, Tori Kelly, Martin Garrix, and Karlie Kloss but also invests in new film and television projects and technology start-ups. Even though he manages some of the most famous people on the planet, Scooter is remarkably down-to-earth and willing to share his life experience. We talk about his own journey in life and what kind of expectations he had, starting from his early high school years.

"I was on the basketball team, I was class president, I was a social kid. People had all these expectations of what I was going to become. They would tell me all the time. When I went to college, it was that pressure of everyone wanting me to become great . . . I worked out of fear. I operated on the idea that what if I didn't live up to their expectations? 'I can't fail. Failure is not an option.' I would work endlessly because I was so scared of failure and not because I was excited for success. That's what drove me. Every time I reached one new achievement, I was on to the next one quickly, because it was never enough. I had a couple of pivotal moments in my life. One was when a buddy of mine died. He was actually killed just after we left a nightclub, and I said to myself, 'I've got to change my life.'"

After that sobering experience, Scooter's drive in life evolved from being one of a fear of failure to a more financial one—hitting the "number."

Scooter says, "I was nineteen when I started my business. When

I was twenty-three I met a guy who had a house, a beautiful family, a dog, and a little whaler boat; I thought he had the perfect life. I said, 'How much money do you need to live this lifestyle?' And he sat me down and told me the amount of money required to live that lifestyle. It's not as much as you think. It takes millions of dollars, but it's not that insane. The number he gave me became my lifetime goal: 'I'm set if I get to that point, and if I double it then I'm beyond set.' I thought I'd work until my fifties to get there."

Scooter recalls the unforgettable moment in his life when he realized he had reached his goal. "When I was twenty-seven years old I was driving down the street in Atlanta when my accountant called. I asked him, 'How much money do I have across all my accounts?' and he named a number higher than my lifetime goal. I was twenty-seven. I said 'Thank you' and hung up the phone. I felt no joy and I started becoming incredibly depressed, because I realized nothing had changed, my life was continuing to go on, nothing had moved."

At that moment of truth, he called on one of the people who had influenced him most in life. "I pulled over to the side of the road and called my dad, and I said, 'I want to tell you my lifetime goal. I've achieved that already. I'm really depressed because nothing changed. I always thought if I got there, I wouldn't feel the pressure, I'd feel joy. But I feel nothing.' My father said one of the wisest things he's ever said to me. He said, 'I want you to do me a favor. I want you to hang up the phone and I want you to think back over the last few years about when you were really happy, and I want you to call me back.' I said, 'What?' and he said, 'Just do it.'"

Scooter continues, "I hung up the phone. I thought about it, called him back two minutes later, and said, 'It's going to sound cheesy, but what really makes me happy are the seemingly small moments that create special experiences for others like playing basketball with old friends, giving away concert tickets, and randomly answering feedback from fans on Facebook.' He said, 'Implement more of that into your life. You can't change what you do or who you are, but you can implement more of the things that actually give you joy into your life.' That was a very big turning point for me. I understood that I don't do this to make money. The joy comes from these things that I implement into that work from the giveback projects that we do to the Saturday morning basketball ritual I have. The joy I have of seeing not only my artists succeed but also the team at SB Projects getting their first platinum plaques and having their own victories. It became about recognizing that joy and implementing more of it into my life."

Another profound realization came with the birth of his and his wife, Yael's, first son, Jagger. "By making life for the first time I understood what death was. My purpose became very real for the first time: put as much of the good things in me into that person as I can until I die. To give as much back to the world as I can before I die, because someday I will no longer exist." He pauses to reflect on the title of this book, *Good Is the New Cool*, and how it relates to the vision of his life. He says, "So we've been talking about what 'cool' is and what is 'good.' Different people can interpret both of those words in many different ways. Is being good doing something you should just do anyway, like being a good father? It's like the famous Chris Rock line, 'Do you want a cookie? For being a good dad?' People are going to interpret 'good' in a different way. I'm hoping to reinforce the idea that you can be successful in this industry and be a good, loving family man."

He continues, "My job isn't to be remembered. My job is to leave a positive impact through my family and my work, because I don't think we get remembered. I think some people get remembered more than others, but eventually we all get forgotten. Your legacy isn't about you; it's about the impact you can leave. I vividly remember sitting there and having this amazing awakening of 'Oh my God, I will not be here someday.' So what is it for? It's to do something worthwhile while I'm here. It's when people say, 'I don't remember Scooter Braun' but they're doing something with their lives in a positive manner, without them even knowing maybe I played a role in that. If I can die knowing that I made that effort, then that's my purpose."

Scooter extends this philosophy to motivating the people who work for him at SB Projects. He says, "It's funny, I feel like I work for them now. I don't need to work anymore. If I chose, I could just stay at home with my family for the rest of my life. There's no amount of money that's going to change my lifestyle. I go to work now to not only see how great we can be but also because there are people who work for me because their paycheck means they can put food in their kid's mouth or a roof over their own head. Just because I've 'won' doesn't mean we've all 'won' yet. So now, the same people who helped me get to where I want to go, now it's my job—I've got to reach down my hand and say, 'OK, let's go. I'm not going anywhere, I'm not going to run off. Now I'm going to reach down and I'll pull you up.'"

This approach may be part of the reason Scooter and his SB Projects team have been so successful in negotiating brand partnerships for his artists. Justin alone has had deals with Adidas, Proactiv, Motorola, and OPI nail polish, and he is currently one of the faces of Calvin Klein. The values that serve as a foundation for SB Projects are on the company's website for everyone to see. They include such aphorisms as "Family is everything," "Superhuman work ethic #hustle and #grind," and "Find your meaning and make it count." Scooter applies these principles to all his artists, helping them translate their emotions into an art form that is loved by people around the world.

He says, "I think that's my job with all of them. I'm not doing it for money. The job is to help them. They're giving one of the most raw art forms a person possibly can to the world, which is their music—they're baring their souls in a way that translates beyond

My job isn't to be
REMEMBERED.

My job is to leave a
**POSITIVE
IMPACT**
through my family
and my work.

SCOOTER BRAUN

language. That's why when we go to countries where people don't speak English, they're singing every lyric to the songs. They're basically pouring out emotions. My job is to help them convey that—and to do so in a way [that makes them] feel comfortable."

Scooter has also always had a strong philanthropic streak in him, something that runs in the family. As mentioned, his brother Adam is the founder of the progressive and successful nonprofit Pencils of Promise, and Justin Bieber has been a loyal supporter, donating his time and energy to raising money for the organization. Bieber has also earmarked funds from some of his licensing deals—his Someday perfume, for example—for Pencils of Promise, as well as donating a dollar from every ticket sold on one of his concert tours to the philanthropic nonprofit. Another little known fact is that Justin is the Make-A- Wish Foundation's number one wish-granter, with over 250 appearances to his name.

Scooter moves on to talk about how he and Justin came up with the theme of "purpose" and how it came to life with the album. "We each came to understand how the theme of purpose was integral to the album in our own ways. As I helped write the song "Purpose," I kept coming back to the major themes in one of my favorite books, Viktor Frankl's *Man's Search for Meaning*. He was a holocaust survivor and psychiatrist who survived through the war, survived Auschwitz, and wrote this book. It talks about the idea that the most powerful thing we have is purpose. And the ones who survived the camps weren't the ones with the most money or the most strength . . . [they were] the ones who had something to live for. When their purpose got taken away, if they were living for their wife and they found out their wife died, they'd quickly die after because they'd lost their purpose."

Man's Search for Meaning has an added layer of meaning for Scooter because his grandparents were also Holocaust survivors. He says, "I started looking at how powerful it was to me and I started thinking about how the best-selling books in the world—like the Bible, for instance—are all based on purpose. I said we should make a song about that because Justin was trying to figure out what this is all for—his purpose. So I started giving Poo Bear, the song's producer and cowriter, all these lines that he built on before showing Justin."

He continues, "Justin loved it. He changed a few words and wrote some personal stuff for him, and that's how the song idea came about. Once he recorded it, he called me up and asked, 'I'm thinking about naming the album *Purpose*. What do you think?' I said, 'It's really amazing for me to hear you say that because that song was very important to me because of [Frankl's] book, but what does it mean to you, because it's your album?' He said, 'I like that it had multiple meanings; I like the fact that it's personal to you. You know, I want it to be personal to my fans.'"

And indeed it has been. Scooter says, "I've been there for his first three . . . shows in this past week, and every single night he plays 'Purpose' last before the encore. And every night he talks and he says, 'Please, if there is anything you take away from this, it's that you should look for the most important thing: purpose,' and he goes, 'I lost mine. I have it now; thanks to all you guys, I found it again. Whatever your purpose is, strive for it.'"

When asked about whether there is a common thread among all the work Scooter does—whether it is managing his talent, his business ventures, or his philanthropic work—Scooter pauses and turns reflective. He says, "There's something my great-grandmother used to say to me, which is, 'Maturity is knowing that your twelve-year-old self is just fine.' You know, this idea of who you always were, it's OK to be that person. I've always been the person—I think Justin has too, we kind of share this—if we go to a comedy, a movie theater . . . we'll laugh, but we'll also turn to see if everyone else is laughing. Everyone laughing won't make us laugh, but we don't get as much joy unless they are. So the common thing between all this is, what's the point of laughing alone? It's this idea of 'sharing joy.'"

WHY WE LOVE THIS EXAMPLE: "Sharing joy." It's as simple as that. Scooter's journey through being driven by the expectations of others, fear of failure, and the desire to hit financial success is an all-too-common one. Sometimes it takes tragedy, like the death of someone close to you, and sometimes it takes profound joy, like the birth of a child, but the clarity always comes at a certain point. True purpose is always in service to somebody or something else; purpose is never for yourself. Scooter's purpose is in service to his family, his artists, and his employees; Justin Bieber's is to his fans and to his craft. By acknowledging their gifts and passions are there to help people other than themselves, they find true meaning and satisfaction.

Aria Finger

CEO, DoSomething.org

Most of us spend the majority of our adult lives trying to figure out what we really give a damn about—our real passions and purpose—and oftentimes, even more years trying to figure out what to do about it. For others—such as Aria Finger, the CEO of DoSomething.org—that clarity came at a very young age. And when you can couple that clarity with a relentless pursuit toward change, it can lead to impact at unprecedented levels.

We spoke with Aria about how DoSomething.org. has turned into one of the largest youth nonprofit organizations for social change in the world, with 5 million members and stellar collaborations with some of the biggest brands in the world.

Ten years after joining DoSomething.org fresh out of college, Aria has had a remarkable rise to become CEO and, more important, has been a driving force in DoSomething.org's ability to harness the power of youth to create widespread global impact.

She says, "The idea of DoSomething.org is that young people want to take action and they want to make the world a better place. They're not actually this group of apathetic people, which is a label that so often gets bestowed upon them. But like any of us, they might not know what to do. They might not know how to make an impact. They might not have time. It's like when you watch a documentary and get all fired up and then think, *Now what?* DoSomething helps take down those barriers and makes it really easy for young people to volunteer and make an impact. We do this by running cause campaigns on issues from homelessness to the environment to sexual assault. Members can run a campaign at their school, and do it with friends.

"We're now the largest organization in the world for young people and social change. We have over 5.2 million members, and our whole goal is to just create the greatest amount of young people doing the greatest amount of good. We really do believe that young people do care about changing the world, and if we can get them to act we can get them to do something, which will make an enormous impact on every cause you can think of from gun violence to climate change to mental health issues to virtually anything. And so every day, we put these 5.2 million young people to work with over 275 campaigns we have on our website. I mean, it's just truly amazing and inspiring, with campaigns on one side and with tens and hundreds of thousands of young people attached to that campaign."

Aria speaks passionately about one of her campaigns, which she worked closely on. It is a great example of how DoSomething.org uses simple solutions coupled with scale to make significant impact. She says, "One of our most famous campaigns is called Teens for

Jeans, and it's centered around collecting and delivering jeans for homeless youth. I launched the campaign over eight years ago when I called homeless shelters and asked, "What do kids need?" We found the number one thing was a pair of jeans. When they go to school, when they get to their job, they need blue jeans for daily clothes, and they can wear them a hundred days in a row. They don't have to wash them. Over a third of the homeless people in the United States are under the age of eighteen. This is a real problem. We asked young people to donate their jeans: one pair, two pairs, and three pairs, as many as you can. Obviously it's a small thing that a young person can do, but if you multiply that by the number of members we had, you know, just last year we collected and donated over 800,000 pairs of jeans, which [were] shipped to almost half of the homeless kids in America. Again it just showed us that a small thing, from a power of scale, can help you make a real impact, I think that's what we focus on at DoSomething is the power of scale. Obviously if you have a campaign that you know impacted twenty or thirty people, that's fantastic, but because we have 5.2 million members, we can affect things at scale and then bring things to another level, which is great."

The ability to create scale is one of the biggest challenges marketers face, particularly at small nonprofits. With big ambitions and limited resources, most nongovernmental organizations (NGOs) struggle to move the needle beyond local impact. What DoSomething.org has done incredibly well is to build an online community of young people that are as passionate about solving problems as the organization is. By seeing young people as powerful allies for change, DoSomething.org has been able to focus its efforts on serving the needs of its members while learning how to create campaigns that effectively activate them. Aria believes that is the key to their success and a lesson for brands as well.

She says, "I think [with] all of our campaigns, we are led by the mantra 'Fight for the user,' and it's painted on our wall at

DoSomething. 'Fight for the user' means everything we do, we consider our users more like members. We work with the celebrities that our members care about and we use communication and technology and tools that our members are using; everything that we do is member-first. I think that has really served us well by being able to serve so well. I think that if more brands did that, the world would be a better place."

That commitment to the needs and best interests of its members has helped DoSomething.org earn the Holy Grail in youth marketing—trust—and, in turn, a valuable role in the lives of young people.

"I think the words that come up a lot [are] 'a trusted resource'; people really trust what DoSomething is bringing to the table," she says. "People thank us all the time and say, 'Because of you, I am now involved.' So I think if we can be that gateway, that entree to launch volunteerism that young people first experience, I feel really good about that, because that's what we want them to do. We want people to come in, find causes they're passionate about, and if they go on to other organizations, we think that's great as long as they're constantly volunteering and making the world a better place."

DoSomething.org also sees corporate brands as powerful allies in social change, and brands see DoSomething.org as a valuable partner for engaging youth in more meaningful ways. "What I think we bring our corporate partners is that young people might not trust corporations, but when they see [they're] partnered with DoSomething on a campaign, then they believe the brands are doing the right thing," Aria says.

To more formally maximize synergies between brands and youth for social change, Aria helped to launch the TMI agency as part of DoSomething.org. In an interview with Cosmopolitan.com, she says, "TMI was an idea I had been bouncing around for a little while. Not only do we see a lot of young people want to participate in social change, we see a lot of brands that want to do it as well. So we use our expertise in marketing and motivating young people, and connect them to brands [such as Keds, Microsoft, and Foot Locker]. All of the additional revenue of TMI goes back into DoSomething. org, allowing us to do more campaigns at even greater scale."[1]

The growing popularity and reputation of the DoSomething. org brand is evident by its recent partnership with the renowned designer Alexander Wang, recognized by *Time* magazine as one of the 100 Most Influential People in 2015. As part of the partnership Wang designed a cool collection of DoSomething-branded clothing that was available for purchase, with 50 percent of the retail price of each piece going to DoSomething.org, in order to raise both funding and awareness.

In classic Wang form, the collection was introduced through a star-studded campaign by talented photographer Steven Klein, who shot a series of portraits of thirty-eight people Wang admires and who influence youth through their work. Each participant donned a piece of the Alexander Wang x DoSomething collection worn in his or her own, personal style. Among the celebrities included were: Kim Kardashian, Kanye West, A$AP Rocky, Kate Moss, Cara Delevingne, the Weeknd, Rod Stewart, Grimes, Kristen Wiig, and Taraji P. Henson.

How did Wang, whom supermodel Karlie Kloss called "the coolest kid in fashion" come to partner with DoSomething.org? Aria Finger says, "Alexander Wang was looking for a charity for his tenth anniversary, and his team gave him a list of different charities [and the ethos of each], and he picked DoSomething. He said [our] ethos [is] what [he] want[s] to live [his] life by. He specifically was

---

1 Aria Finger. "Get That Life: How I Became the CEO of DoSomething.org." Interview by Heather Wood Rudolph. *Cosmopolitan*. December 21, 2015. http://www.cosmopolitan.comcareer/news/a50550/get-that-life-aria-finger-do-something-dot-org-ceo/.

interested in the fact that we didn't focus on one cause, we focused on many, that was one of the reasons he liked us because we didn't stand for just the environment or for racial justice, it was all of those, and obviously Alexander Wang is a huge brand so he was excited about the fact that we understood young people and were activating young people."

With projects like this, Aria understands as well as anyone the immense power pop culture can play in social change work; as a matter of fact, it's in the DNA of the brand. "I think pop culture is important," she says. "DoSomething was originally founded by Andrew Shue because he wanted to make community service as cool as sports; he wanted it to be part of everyday culture and not something you do once in a while for a school project or for whatever it may be. I think as pop culture has been able to normalize so many things, it's been able to sort of push forward gay rights, push forward racial justice agendas, all these things."

However, Aria is also cautious of nonprofits using celebrities and the cachet of cool aimlessly. She says, "I think you need to be careful, [because there are] situations where the 'thing' that's 'cool' is not necessarily actually good for the world. Because there's a lot of greenwashing in the entire social-space community where some people say, 'Well, it looks good' or 'It looks buzzy,' which doesn't make an impact, and you just want to make sure that your goals and vision are aligned; you're not just doing cool things, if it's not impactful."

Although it's clear through DoSomething.org's partnerships Aria is supportive of brands and celebrities looking to affect society in positive ways, she recommends they stick to their strengths. "I think one of the trends that I don't love is seeing celebrities and brands create their own nonprofit," she says. "I think sometimes they neglect to understand how difficult it is to run a complete organization. And they are not experts [and] might not do a good job; we want these organizations to have more longevity. . . . So I think there really is a need for partnership and really figuring out what the celebrities do best, what the brands do best, [and what] the NGOs do best, and then when you put them all together, you'll have the next creative item. It doesn't help anyone when the NGOs are creating clothing and celebrities are creating NGOs."

She continues, "I think NGOs know best how to solve problems. They understand the needs of the people they are serving. A great example is Mark Zuckerberg. When he gave back $100 million to a Newark school, they wasted it; they didn't do the right thing with it at all, because Zuckerberg himself didn't understand that landscape, and [he and his people] didn't ask other stakeholders, they didn't ask the local NGOs and the community. So again I think that NGOs would know how to solve problems the best. So what does DoSomething do best? Far and away, we know how to activate young people. We might not be the best content creators or we may not be the best at any of those other things, but we can activate young people; that's what we do, and that's our best product."

We also talked about what the most important first steps are in creating a successful partnership. Aria says, "I feel goals need to be aligned. If one person's goals are media impressions and the other person's goals are a number of people concentrated on social media, no matter what, that's not going to be a good partnership because you're each striving for other things. So I think goal alignments are really the key, understanding the other person's core competency and then just communication—making sure, just as in any partnership, relationship, whatever. Communication is essential."

As someone who realized early in life that she wanted to make the world more fair and just, Aria found the perfect place to work toward that goal. Now a CEO, she works to ensure that purpose is at the heart of all that DoSomething does. "Everything we do is purpose," she says. "As much as possible, [we] bake it in from the beginning, and the organization is only as good as the sum of its parts, so make sure you're hiring people who are there for the right reasons, make sure you are hiring people because of the purpose, and then if you do that, then you're on the way there."

WHY WE LOVE THIS EXAMPLE: We love this example because it shows the magnetic powers of passion and purpose. When you know and share what you really give a damn about, it draws you closer, in unexpected ways, to other people and organizations that care about the same things. In this case, DoSomething.org's purpose of creating cool ways for young people to help make the world a better place has attracted brands, causes, celebrities, and more than 5 million young people who want the same thing, including one young person who, ten years later, has become the organization's CEO.

Matthew Clough

Founder, Stone & Cloth

The data is clear: 75 percent of the global workforce will be millennials by 2025—and 80 percent of them say they want a job that doesn't just pay the bills but has a purpose that matches their passion. Here's the story of one inspirational young entrepreneur who started his own company in order to provide others with a place where they didn't have to "choose between purpose and a paycheck."

Sometimes the journey to purpose can start in the most unexpected of places. Matthew Clough's journey began when he was climbing Mount Kilimanjaro, of all places. A conversation Matthew had with his porter, Benson, led to the realization that Benson didn't have enough money to put his child through school. Out of that journey came Stone & Cloth, a fashion brand with elegant bags and products (the very first of which was called the Benson in honor of the man who inspired him). Their profits partially fund children's education in Africa, via a partnership with the Knock Foundation, which gives grants in countries such as Tanzania. The brand is loved by fashion blogs and boutiques, and is starting to gain fans and followers across the world (and has also collaborated with brands such as Scion and Target).

Matthew could have gone in any number of directions for his career; in fact, he started his career as a data retargeter (he basically worked for a software company that figured out people's online shopping habits and served them relevant ads). But his moment of realization in Tanzania has left him happy and fulfilled about his sense of purpose in life. He says, "Truly, deep down inside . . . everyone wants to be part of something bigger than themselves. Everyone wants the opportunity to help others, [to] make other people's lives [better]. But until recently it was really difficult to find that sweet spot between making a living and helping other people. Because of traumatic events like Katrina, 9/11, [and] the economic downturn in 2008, we have learned to empathize with other people. We're all connected, and we all need to help each other."

In a time of recession and economic uncertainty, the safe bet would have been to take a corporate job with a steady paycheck, but Matthew chose otherwise. He talks about how the rise of social businesses like his gives millennials another option. "You don't need to make a choice like before," he says. "You don't have to sacrifice a paycheck or a health-care plan—where if you took the job you had a paycheck but no sense of purpose. There's a lightbulb going off over people's heads: 'I can still make a steady paycheck *and* do something useful with my time.'"

Matthew says he was lucky enough to intern at TOMS (the shoe company that was one of the pioneers in the social business space), where he learned many valuable lessons. He learned to "imbue the product with meaning," he says. "The people wearing your product have a trigger: 'I'm doing some good when I'm wearing it. I'm doing something positive while doing it.' People now wear TOMS like they wear Nikes."

He also acknowledges how important it is to follow "Cool" as a driver of his success. "Cool is the price of entry. The importance of design, fashion, and style is a part of the success. As customers became more sophisticated and demanded quality in socially conscious products, talking about why you are doing what you're doing is not enough, you have to keep up with market trends."

Some larger companies have also entered into this space—notably the footwear giant Skechers who have launched a blatant rip-off of TOMS called BOBS. Matthew is very diplomatic in his view of these moves by larger corporations, saying, "I think it's great that socially conscious start-ups are being noticed by larger brands and it's causing them to do something responsibly. But they should just do it well. Social business is such a fragile category that if large companies blundered into that space, it could destroy it."

Matthew's belief is that start-ups like his are the predecessor to a major shift in business itself. "I totally think social business is the future of business," he says. "Those companies with a deeper sense of purpose will be much more agile in finding a model that succeeds. As time progresses, markets will start changing faster and the companies who do keep up will be the ones who survive. That's what gets me out of bed in the morning."

TRULY, DEEP DOWN INSIDE ... EVERYONE WANTS TO BE PART OF SOMETHING BIGGER THAN THEMSELVES.

MATTHEW CLOUGH

WHY WE LOVE THIS EXAMPLE: To millennials like Matthew, the smart companies are the ones that have a purpose, which translates into the products they create for customers. They provide authenticity and meaning in a world filled with noise. It's a backlash against materialism, against excess, against celebrity culture, and against being manipulated. And brands that have a clear sense of purpose become not only attractive brands to buy but also attractive places to work. Unless you can imbue your product and brand with genuine purpose, you won't attract the finest talent, or customers who believe in what you stand for.

2.
FIND YOUR ALLIES

Once you've found purpose, you next must find allies: people and organizations whose purpose intersects with yours. We look at how brands (with their resources and reach) are partnering with nonprofits (which provide in-depth knowledge and problem-solving skills) and Architects of Cool (who provide the cultural spotlight and storytelling skills to mobilize millions). We'll provide some insight on how you can build powerful platforms and movements that connect and inspire on a large scale.

In this section, see how Jenifer Willig built a community of allies during her time as CMO of Product (RED)—the social-good juggernaut founded by Bono—and how she's applying what she learned there to her new venture, Whole World Water, which works with hotels to generate profits for clean-water projects around the world. We dive into the world of Greg Propper, cofounder of Propper Daley, as he builds alliances between writers, directors, and artists in Hollywood to drive social attitudinal and behavioral change. And Ryan Cummins, the cofounder of Omaze tells us about how he partners with allies such as J.J. Abrams, Robert Downey Jr., and John Legend to give fans once-in-a-lifetime experiences while raising millions of dollars for causes.

Jenifer Willig

Founder, Motive and Whole World Water

The idea that brands could make money from supporting causes, and not feel guilty about making a profit, was not always a common one. One of the pivotal moments was the launch of the Project (RED) (also referred to simply as "(RED)") platform, founded in 2006 by U2 frontman Bono and Bobby Shriver to raise awareness and funds to fight against HIV/AIDs. It trailblazed a new type of cause marketing—one that made it more palatable and easy for brands to get involved. It built a mighty coalition of brands from every category: Nike, Apple, American Express, Coke, Starbucks, Armani, the Gap—and even got competing brands (such as Converse and Nike) to set aside their rivalry for the common good.

One person who has a deep understanding of how to work with the right allies is Jenifer Willig, who had a ringside seat at (RED)'s journey as their first chief marketing officer. During Willig's four-year tenure, (RED) succeeded in raising $185 million and became a powerhouse global brand with an active social following of more than 2.5 million advocates. She is now the founder of Motive, a social innovation consultancy, as well as one of the cofounders of Whole World Water, a campaign to unite the hospitality and tourism industries to help provide clean and safe water to people around the world.

Friendly, open, and disarmingly honest, Jenifer talks about how she got started. She says, "I spent my career in advertising, I was feeling jaded . . . and in 2007, I got a call from a friend who said, 'They're looking for someone to professionalize (RED).' I was never a volunteer, I worked all the time. I wasn't an AIDS activist at the time, though I've certainly been converted!'"

The genius of (RED) was that it allowed cause marketing to get out of the doom and gloom and find a new tonality, which allowed brands not to feel guilty about making money from it. Jenifer explains, "It was something (RED) did, as far as AIDS: not portraying it as it had been shown before, as a death sentence, and showing people that AIDS is a preventable and treatable disease; and that it's about living, not dying. That changed the whole perspective and tone—you could have fun with it, you could be cool and irreverent and quirky . . . all of that stuff that when you have a rock star who has founded the organization, you should be able to embrace."

Jenifer knew the importance of making sure the products (RED) sold "Led with the Cool." She says, "One of the things we learned was that (RED) couldn't sell a bad product; even in 2006, the idea of buying the scratchy sweater because it did good was not going to work as a sustainable business model. There were a lot of people who came to us where we had to push to get their top-selling product. Some people slapped a (RED) logo on a product that wasn't selling well, and it still wouldn't sell—not because people didn't agree with the issue; they didn't want to buy a bad product! And I think that's the evolution of how smart customers are. People are much smarter than we marketers give them credit for. . . . You can't put lipstick on a pig."

Jenifer is now applying that same learning to the Whole World Water campaign, which she explained to us, saying, "A hotel or restaurant joins the global marketing campaign; we provide all of the collateral. Step two is that they agree to provide still and sparkling water to their guests in beautiful reusable glass bottles (designed by Yves Béhar) that we provide. And step three is they agree to give 10 percent of their proceeds from those sales to the Whole World Water fund; 100 percent of that money is used to fund clean and safe water initiatives around the world."

What makes this different from (RED) is that this is a truly global initiative; Whole World Water has members from all over the world, from the Maldives and Mauritius to Africa, Europe, and the United States. And they allow members to earmark the funds they raise for their local communities, which means the funds aren't going to some anonymous project.

Jenifer's passion for the project comes through loud and clear. "There's a billion people living today without access to clean and safe water; it is truly a global crisis that's happening. We have one hundred members so far and seven projects on the ground. It's a win-win-win-win: they reduce their costs by not selling commercially bottled water, they increase their revenue because the margins are much lower, they're reducing their plastic waste significantly, and collectively we can raise money for clean and safe water initiatives."

Her parting advice to marketers: "Find a way to make an impact that is tied to the business; there is nothing wrong with the way you give back also being tied to your business. There are so many models out there, so many innovative ways to impact the business, whether

THERE ARE SO MANY

MODELS OUT THERE,

WHETHER YOU ARE A RETAIL BRAND OR A LUXURY BRAND,

that haven't been thought of as yet.

JENIFER WILLIG

you are a retail brand or a luxury brand, that haven't been thought of as yet. We can't stick to the way things have been done to impact how quickly the world is changing. Businesspeople bring a really strong perspective to social innovation that hasn't been there before. The nonprofit space is a wonderful space and very necessary, but they aren't businesspeople. The beautiful thing I am seeing is that the nonprofits are looking to hire businesspeople to create models and revenue streams that are going to grow the impact they are having. As marketers or business people, we bring a really unique perspective to solving large social issues.'

WHY WE LOVE THIS EXAMPLE: Jenifer's experience with (RED) led to her finding her own area of passion (clean water), but it also led to her finding a unique model that worked for her particular organizational model. There isn't just a one-size-fits-all approach that works for every brand in every category at every stage of life. So keep searching until you find the model that's right for you and your brand. Do small beta tests to see if it works before scaling it, so the organization has time to adjust and implement any information it learns from the tests.

Greg Propper

Cofounder, Propper Daley

The power of Hollywood to influence public opinion has long been clear: From getting the American public involved in WW2 to countless PSAs warning against the dangers of smoking, drunk driving, teen pregnancy, and the like. But in recent years, nonprofits and public-health officials have started taking an even more sophisticated approach, one that goes beyond standard tactics to create measurable, quantifiable social change by harnessing the power of pop culture.

So you're sitting on your couch, binge-watching *Orange Is the New Black* on Netflix. One of the female characters who is in prison has a visit with her baby and the baby's father. As the father and baby leave, the female inmate calls out to the father to make sure he reads, talks, and sings to the baby, warning him that otherwise there may be developmental issues. You didn't know it, but that was the handiwork of Greg Propper, one of the cofounders of Propper Daley, a "social impact agency" that works with culture creators in Hollywood to create positive social change.

Greg has a long history of public service in the political and nonprofit world, from working for the Democratic Congressional Campaign Committee in Washington to serving as managing director for Be the Change. We caught up with him about his journey, which has led him to collaborating with the Clinton Foundation on combating childhood illiteracy, with Bradley Cooper on changing the perception of veterans, and with John Legend on the campaign to end mass incarceration. He talked about some of the dangers facing social entrepreneurs that Be the Change tries to solve.

He says, "There's this concept called the social entrepreneurs' trap: as a social entrepreneur you get so caught up running your organization, managing your staff, managing your board, [and] raising money that these brilliant, disruptive, innovative social entrepreneurs who went into this work to change the world end up spending all of their time trying to run and scale organizations that ultimately are difficult to scale—sometimes at the expense of changing systems. And so Be the Change was meant to be a platform for these social entrepreneurs to come together on issues that [they] were stuck [on] and try and get them on track."

To put it another way—Be the Change was essentially about finding allies who could help you with the back-end infrastructure of running and scaling an organization. Greg says, "It was interesting learning actually with our first campaign. We helped, along with our coalition, get passed a piece of legislation in the first one hundred days of the Obama administration called the Edward M. Kennedy Serve America Act, which authorized the expansion for AmeriCorps from 75,000 to 250,000 people a year, which was the largest expansion of national service in this country since the Great Depression."

Despite this success, Greg realized there were other challenges that came with turning the legislation into action. "But to this day it has not been funded, and part of our insight of that time was we hadn't done a really great job with regards to the public. We had reached the president and editorial boards and NGOs, but we hadn't done a good enough job building public will for this idea of service here. We hadn't popularized or normalized this idea of a year of service as a part of what it means to grow up in this country. So when it came time for members of Congress to appropriate funds, there were not enough young people knocking down their doors. So there was sort of this wake-up call for us that we needed to spend a lot more time on the demand side in addition to the supply side, and we needed to do a better job at essentially culture change."

That was the impetus for Greg to move to Los Angeles and start a new chapter in his life, working to create large-scale social change. He says, "I moved to L.A. to open our West Coast office for Be the Change, and we started working with a lot of folks in the entertainment industry, a number of high-profile celebrities. And at the time they all were saying the same things. It was 2009 and the economy had collapsed and I think most of these celebrities—like everybody else in the country—wanted to feel like they were doing something that was moving the needle. And I think for many of them, they felt like they were spending a little time here, a little money there, but not actually getting anything done."

Greg talks about how he saw the traditional approach to leveraging celebrity and fame to create social change was in need of an update. "At the time in L.A., if you were an A-list celebrity or an artist/

influencer, and you wanted to create a measurable outcome-oriented change in the world, you had to either hire a nonprofit advisor, who might tell you how to give your money, or a political advisor who will help you shape policy, or a publicist or a marketing firm, all of whom [have] a role to play. But in reality, oftentimes when you're trying to create measurable outcome-oriented change, that is going to require all of those strategies, right? It's just the way change happens in the world. And so our idea at the time, almost five years ago, was to launch a 'social-impact agency.' To try to create a holistic, strategic, one-stop shop for individuals, organizations, [and] companies who are looking to create measurable outcome-oriented change in the world."

A more discerning and savvy public audience also demanded a new approach that prioritized authenticity and real change, as opposed to surface optics. Greg says, "Yes, I think part of it is a growing understanding in general about sort of the complexities but also the need for serious social change. And so part of it, I think, is an acknowledgment among the entertainment and creative community that they have a responsibility, and also the ability, to create real significant change. But I also think the public is more discerning, and the younger generation in particular is more likely to affiliate themselves or to support brands, individuals, or others who share their values, but [they] are also more able and more likely to see through approaches that are inauthentic. I think there's a sort of accountability that comes with a more discerning public."

Greg talked about the importance of moving the public along a continuum from awareness of an issue to attitudinal change to finally behavioral change. "I think there is a default in the social-change field to go right to awareness or just jump right to tactics, when in reality if you want to create real culture change, I think it requires a requisite level of awareness but also behavior and attitude change," Greg says. "So when we work with our clients, nonprofits, individuals, brands, we lead them to a process where we say, 'Awareness plus attitude change plus behavioral change equals X. Where are you strong? And where do we need to do some work? And then how do we more surgically deploy the assets of culture to help achieve that?'"

He continues, "The issue of obesity, for example: generally people are aware that if you eat poorly you're going to gain weight. But you still eat poorly because of peer pressure, stress, or you live in a food desert. Then it's not about awareness, it is about 'How do we use culture to shift people's behaviors and attitudes?' Smoking was another example, right? We had to be aware that smoking causes cancer before [we could] get people to think it was a bad idea and then actually get them to quit. So a part of what we are trying to think about with our clients is how to use celebrity and culture differently to incentivize attitudes and behavior shifts."

One of Propper Daley's recent successes has been around the issue of ensuring veterans are portrayed in a positive light in popular culture. Greg says, "We ran a veterans campaign for example, called Got Your 6. And we launched last year with an event with [first lady Michelle] Obama and Bradley Cooper, something called 6 Certified, where we are working with writers' rooms for television shows and films, and help[ing] introduce it to real-life veterans. And we're helping them understand that not all veterans are heroes, and not all veterans are broken, but most of them are somewhere in between. And then every year we certify somewhere between six and twenty television and film projects that accurately and reasonably portray veterans. And we do a perception-shift study every year in partnership with a research firm in DC to monitor how the portrayals of film and television actually shift the way that the public is perceiving veterans. How am I as an employer, or as a neighbor, thinking about and perceiving veterans as they are coming out? Am I perceiving them as unemployed? Homeless? Having suffered abuse? Perceiving them as heroes on a pedestal, or am I perceiving them as someone who is a lot like myself? Because we know that if they perceive veterans more positively, they'll be more likely to hire them or likely to help them create a successful life."

Building on the theme of "Find Your Allies," Greg talks about how one of the most powerful strategies was to ensure that like-minded organizations, driven by a common purpose, didn't compete with each other but rather streamlined their approach to drive greater success. "So there's a lot of talk lately about collective impact," he says. "How do you bring together a lot of different organizations, brands, [and] individuals who are working towards similar goals but maybe competing for resources, working independently to get them to align around common goals? And I think two of the things that can incentivize that really well [are] one, celebrity, and two, money. So there's a role for celebrity and entertainment to incentivize collaboration amongst a fragmented field. One of the best examples I think is the Entertainment Industry Foundation, who we work with, and their Stand Up to Cancer campaign. They went to the cancer research field and said, 'What are the barriers that are keeping you from doing your work?' Things like, 'People aren't doing clinical trials fast enough' or, 'They are not sharing information.' They took the idea and went to a bunch of brands and funders and said, 'We are going to raise hundreds of millions of dollars. We are going to do a national telecast every two years with every single celebrity in the world.' And then they went to the field and said, 'If you want access to this money, you have to really follow these things,' right? 'You have to do faster trials, and you're going to share your research,' and they ended up creating this Cancer Dream Team. It's an example of one of the most powerful uses of celebrity and brand and funding to incentivize systemic change and collaboration."

Another approach to "Find Your Allies" that Greg highlights is the sterling work being done by artist and activist John Legend around his particular focus on ending mass incarceration. Greg says, "We get to work with John Legend and [his] Free America campaign. John is brilliant, right? He is so smart about this and how to use his profile.

One of the things that he is trying to do is, he did a listening and learning tour of prisons and [brought] policy makers with him. Once he went to the women's prison in Washington State and brought with him one hundred leaders of the labor movement who have traditionally been somewhat resistant to criminal justice reform. But the facts of a broken criminal justice system for labor are that many of their members or potential members are behind bars, or are members who are working in prisons in substandard conditions. So instead of building a barrier, he said, 'Let's go together,' which is kind of amazing.

And in regard to how brands can get involved, Greg talks about an imaginative partnership between Airbnb and Service Year Alliance. (The Service Year Alliance was the result of the merger between the Franklin Project, ServiceNation, and the Service Year Exchange (SYx), and is a joint venture between Be the Change and the Aspen Institute.) "There's a coalition of organizations focused on national service, called the Service Year Allianc," Greg says. "They have been working with brands; one of the most interesting was that they partnered with Airbnb to offer two weeks of free housing to new members while they look for permanent housing. I thought it was a really interesting example [of] how a relevant company can support an unlikely cause, but also how the company or brands can use what is authentic to them and use their assets in a really interesting and productive way."

WHY WE LOVE THIS EXAMPLE: The work that Greg and his team do builds powerful coalitions between Architects of Cool—such as writers, directors, actors, and musicians—and nonprofits such as the Clinton Foundation and Service Year Alliance in ways that can create seismic shifts in popular culture and help drive public opinion. It is a model many organizations, including brands, can learn much from as they find ways to harness the power of pop culture to help solve the world's problems.

Ryan Cummings

Cofounder, Omaze

Millennials overwhelmingly say they value experiences over material objects. Perhaps it's a legacy of living through the 2008 financial crisis, when they saw their parents' generation lose homes, stocks, and bonds after decades of saving and toil. Perhaps it's just a more enlightened approach that comes from being born into a world full of material abundance but short on profound experiences. In this chapter we meet Ryan Cummings, the founder of Omaze, a platform that allows ordinary people to access extraordinary experiences—and raises a ton of money for good causes in the meantime.

There's a saying that while necessity may be the mother of invention, frustration may be the father of creativity. It certainly was the case when Ryan Cummings and his best friend since college, Matt Pohlson, were driving home one night after attending a charity auction for the Boys & Girls Club. One of the prizes that evening had been a chance to play basketball with their childhood hero, Magic Johnson. But as often happens, the bidding for the experience soon went sky-high and out of reach for Ryan and Matt. They discussed the essential unfairness of charity auctions and how they were only accessible to the wealthy, and out of that frustration was born the idea for Omaze.

"Because it was only available at auction, only the wealthy individuals in the room actually even had a shot; and it was cleared for $15,000," Ryan says. "We were driving home that night and we were like, 'That's a loss for everybody.' It was a loss for Magic Johnson, this global icon who's spending his time and energy to support the Boys & Girls Club; he should be making so much more money and raising so much more awareness for them. It's a loss for the Boys & Girls Club with that opportunity, and a loss for the fans who would love a way to be able to engage Magic Johnson and support something he cares about . . . and have a shot at this dream experience. And that's where really the idea for Omaze came about."

Omaze's model is simple: they raise money for charities by offering once-in-a-lifetime experiences that anyone can bid on for as low as ten dollars. Some of these experiences range from John Legend singing at your wedding to having the "best night of your life" with Robert Downey Jr., which involved skydiving, fine dining, getting fitted for a tux or a ball gown, and then going to the *Avengers* premiere.

Their most successful project to date has been for *Star Wars: The Force Awakens*, for which they collaborated with J.J. Abrams to give fans a chance to win a part in the new film, as well as visits to the set. Bad Robot, Lucasfilm, and Disney created a brand-new philanthropic initiative called Force for Change for the *Star Wars* franchise that benefited the UNICEF Innovation Labs and raised $4.2 million. By opening access to the millions of *Star Wars* fans, they unlocked a tremendous amount of value—and raised far more money than if they had done a traditional private charity action.

Their hypothesis is that traditional philanthropy, a $240 billion dollar market, is incredibly inefficient. Just like Kickstarter eliminated the friction associated with funding a project, Omaze unlocked the potential for broader fund-raising. Filmmakers, musicians, and celebrities raise more money than ever before for the causes they care about—and in the process also generate a tremendous amount of awareness.

We caught up with Ryan to talk a little bit about his journey and how the forces of "Good" and "Cool" now intersect in the expectations of the way people do business. He says, "Business could succeed historically without necessarily having to have greater consciousness associated with whether or not this business was done in a way deemed 'good'; but in today's global marketplace, it's almost impossible to separate the input, process, and outcome of the business from society. And so business is largely linked to whether it's being done in a way that is 'good,' whereas 'good' might have been an afterthought historically. The success of business today is predicated on that higher or elevated level [of] consciousness, and so when you look at it that way, it's not that it's just being done in a cool way, but [with] cool people doing business."

Today success in business relies on having a deeper level of wisdom and insight, the ability to understand the multidimensional way that successful businesses operate. By getting out of the short-term focus on profits at any cost, and realizing long-term growth depends on a more enlightened way of doing business than ever before, businesses are future-proofing themselves for survival. This enlightened approach has permeated the world of the Architects of Cool who have become Omaze's greatest allies.

Ryan says, "What we really started seeing is that these . . . people that are celebrities, influencers, icons that we had an opportunity to work with are really the ones who are most innovative, are early adopters of 'storytelling for purpose'; but they also are the ones who actually care the most about whatever it is that purpose is associated with. We live in a world where, more and more, what you do with your time and your influence is a part of how much influence people want to give you; what you actually do as a celebrity with the energy and the spotlight and the collective attention you are given ends up becoming reciprocal into how much more attention you are given."

It is testimony to the fact that these Architects of Cool are realizing their legacy has to be more than their last movie or their last album; it is about leaving the planet in better shape than they found it. Ryan talks about some of the numbers behind the successful fund-raising campaigns they have carried out to date. He says, "So we focus primarily on campaigns where we know we can raise more than they can do at auctions; we raise anywhere between five to twenty times versus the experiences raised at auctions. And if you take a couple of examples of experiences we've done in that similar vein—the chance to go on a date with George Clooney to walk the red carpet (that was before he got married to Amal, by the way), the chance to ride a tank and crush things with Arnold Schwarzenegger, the chance to have the best night of your life with Robert Downey Jr., or the opportunity to be in *Star Wars: Episode VII*— at auction those would typically raise between $25,000 to . . . $100,000 if you have a really loaded room. Through Omaze those ended up raising $1.1 million, $1.2 million, $2 million, and $4.26 million, respectively. So in each one of those cases, they raised over a million bucks for different charities."

Ryan talks about how this evolution in their model has led

to them pivoting away from replacing charity auctions to creating something brand new. "We don't see ourselves as a competitor to charity auctions; we see ourselves right now as the most innovative online fund-raising platform," Ryan says. "We are building a brand-new marketplace for fund-raising that makes giving fun and easy, and allows all of these different cultural icons to [tell stories] about their causes, about the things that they care about."

The attractiveness of the model has meant Omaze is now hearing from a lot of brands that are keen to participate in a way that augments their traditional marketing. Ryan says, "We held off brands for quite a long time—we made a conscious decision that we didn't want to be a digital agency—but in the process of doing that we had brands come to us. We've done a couple of campaigns. One very large one was Coke and (RED), where they saw that [by] partnering up with Omaze, they could basically get out the messaging of Coke in a very different way. In a way that's ancillary to their traditional marketing, but in ways that are more authentic and genuine to the philanthropic aims of the brand. And so that's something we've been excited about: finding ways in which the brand is able to partner with cultural ambassadors, icons, celebrities to continue to put up once-in-a-lifetime experiences that engage people in an authentic and genuine way around brands."

Similar to brands, Omaze has also developed really close relationships with the nonprofits that have been the beneficiaries of the programs they have run; and Ryan alludes to the fact that the next evolution they are working on is designed to empower them even more. "We cannot wait until we can service all the nonprofits that are coming to us," he says. "Because of the nature of the business right now, we are working with the best influencers, but we are committed to building a tool that will help all the nonprofits, 501(c)(3)s, schools, congregations around the country—basically take the core assets of Omaze and fundraise themselves and have that model.

Ultimately [we] want [there] to be a philanthropic layer to all experiences, to really make sure that people know giving is fun and easy because of Omaze. So we are really excited about that opportunity."

Omaze's for-profit model (taking a fixed 20 percent of the money raised) allows them to be sustainable and create a business model that isn't dependent on donations or having to do their own fundraising. Their thirty-five-person team based in Los Angeles is constantly on the lookout for new partnerships—not that there is any shortage of cultural icons knocking on their door. For that share of revenue, they put together a full end-to-end program from designing and executing the experiences to creating the campaign, assets, and content to amplify the message.

Ryan expands on the benefits of Omaze having a for-profit model, saying, "We see that everything that goes along with being a for-profit business puts Omaze in a position to change the way charities can raise money, and can raise them significantly more amounts of money and awareness than through the traditional models. The way in which governments are defunding programs for education, health services, for veterans; the limitations that charities face around how they are able to fund raise and how they are able to market around their fund-raising; there are just certain constraints that we think inhibit the nonprofit space from being able to capture its full potential. And by taking aspects of a for-profit model and putting a company in a position where we can partner with nonprofits, we think there is a larger opportunity."

This new model for solving problems seems to resonate well with Omaze's audience, whom Ryan believes to have accepted this novel approach. "I think by and large they've fully adopted this," he says. "I think so long as we continue to be very transparent about how the model works, consumers are smart, supporters are smart; collectively intelligen[ce] really wins at the end of the day. So as long as the company is transparent about what it is that it's doing, and constantly engaging and communicating with the audience, then the audience will usually respond in an honest way as well."

A big part of Omaze's success is letting the creative partners come up with their own concepts and unlock their own creativity in service of their causes. And that creativity is what takes it from a standard meet-and-greet with Arnold Schwarzenegger to being able to ride around in a tank with him and crush things that raised $1.2 million (or having him dress up as the Terminator and scare the living daylights out of unaware tourists on Hollywood Boulevard, which generated 26 million views on YouTube).

Ryan talks about the importance of the model firing on all cylinders—great influencers, great storytelling, great experiences, and great content—as a direct correlation to the success of each initiative. He says, "I think that we were firm in our belief that the storytelling was going to accomplish the awareness part, the impact just wasn't there to match it. Now we are seeing that we've developed a model where the impact can at least be in line—or, over time, greater than—just the storytelling for awareness, so that's definitely been the evolution of our path. At the end of the day, it's about bringing people together in a way that they are excited to engage and learn and support, so the experience becomes a really critical element. There is not one piece you can focus on; it's all of them in concert with each other. You just had an awesome experience but you really didn't have a good piece of content around it, then you are not really reaching the maximum people possible. You could just have a really great cause, but [if] you don't have a great experience and storytelling, then you're not hitting it. You know you can't have good storytelling without a great influencer, experience, and cause. So it's really pulling all those things together in a way that then becomes exciting for the most amount of people possible."

It is this dedication to making sure all the pieces of the puzzle fit together that has also led to Omaze's dual markers for success—raising funds *and* raising awareness.

Ryan says, "I mean, all of them matter. You know, if we were to put on a campaign and only two people heard about it but it raised a million bucks . . . that wouldn't be a success for us. But if we were to put on a campaign and a million people heard about it and it [only] raised two bucks, that wouldn't be a success for us either. Success for us is we are authentically and genuinely telling the story of the cause, but doing so in a way that really allows the influencer an opportunity to shine all of their influence on that cause, and as a result raise a lot of awareness. And by raising awareness, you end up raising funds. So we are serving everyone."

The more we dived deeper into Omaze, we realized that they may be one of the best examples of the primary thesis of this book: that today it is possible to "Make Money and Do Good by Harnessing the Power of Cool." Their platform has been designed to serve all their stakeholders—the causes, the celebrities, the community—in a win-win-win model. At the heart of this lies a very clear organizational purpose.

Of this, Ryan says, "Our higher purpose as a company is that 'we serve world changers.' And we see that the world changers are the influencers, they are the causes, they are also the beneficiaries of the cause, and they are the communities and supporters all coming to help to support this whole campaign. So we are just there to serve everybody, and we feel when all the boxes get checked that the supporters, contributors, and fans are getting the experiences that they are excited about, they are getting a lot of content and the information that they are excited about. And the influencers feel like they are getting the maximum reach for their effort, and in return on their effort, in the form of funds raised for that cause. So it's about helping everybody."

The clarity of this vision not only underscores the importance of a higher purpose that guides the company but shows you what it is like when a perfectly designed purpose serves all the stakeholders of the company just as much as it serves the needs of the company itself. Ryan talks frankly about how much time they dedicated not only to crafting that purpose but making sure it became a living, breathing part of the company culture. He says, "We spent probably the first six months of the company, before we even launched, making sure we had a higher purpose that we really believed in. Everybody knows our mission, which is to build a community that leverages the power of storytelling and technology to transform lives. And those aren't just words to us; that's really what we're all about. Where else would I have the opportunity to engage with the most influential people on the planet towards something that's truly, authentically good, and in a way that is still fun? This is a dream opportunity in that regard."

WHY WE LOVE THIS EXAMPLE: Omaze has created a win-win-win model: fans get access to extraordinary experiences for low rates, the Architects of Cool get to leverage their fame and creativity to raise orders of magnitude more money than traditional auctions, and nonprofits benefit from the millions of dollars raised. Omaze now does more than 200 different auctions a year, and has plans to build its platform out to be used by any school, charity, or organization— as well as plans to extend the idea globally (imagine the potential of Bollywood superstars or Chinese film icons using this in their gigantic markets). The force is definitely strong with them.

3.
THINK CITIZENS, NOT CONSUMERS

We believe that when brands think of people only as consumers, they are condemned to have a narrow relationship with them. But when they think of people as citizens, they can suddenly see the range of passions and causes they care about, and spot opportunities for collaboration that will lead to a relationship that is "transformational not transactional."

In this section, we meet the passionate creative director Fernanda Romano, and talk about a life-changing project she created with the paint brand Dulux and hundreds of communities around the world; we meet the "inspiring troublemaker" Ahmen, who works for a nonprofit by day and is a rapper by night, blending his gifts for social entrepreneurship and social commentary; and we also talk to the hypercool artist Aerosyn-Lex Mestrovic about the unique role he feels artists and art have in being able to spark positive social change.

Fernanda Romano

Founder, Malagueta Group

When exploring the idea of this new model for marketing, we asked ourselves a question: is this model only valid in countries with developed economies and more sophisticated customers? The answer is no. In fact, we believe it may be even more valuable in the developing world, which has a disproportionate share of complicated issues (climate change, social inequality) and also the opportunity to leapfrog old models of thinking and go straight into this new paradigm. One inspiring example is how the paint brand Dulux found a way to energize communities around the world from Capetown to Ho Chi Minh City to Rio.

IF PEOPLE WEREN'T PART OF IT, THEY [WOULD] HAVE NO OWNERSHIP OF IT.

Fernanda Romano

Dulux had a problem. The brand realized they were in a category—paint—that was rapidly becoming commoditized and needed a way to create an emotional connection with its customers. They carried out an intensive program of both internal and external workshops to find out what Dulux and the product it was selling meant to people. And the answer they found was somewhat surprising: color meant emotion. And paint became a way of helping people express those emotions—happiness, optimism, calmness.

Finding their purpose opened a whole new territory for Dulux to explore in their marketing. They realized they had the opportunity to bring color—and optimism—into the lives of their customers. By treating them as citizens and not just consumers, they realized they had an opportunity to engage and collaborate with them in their communities in an unprecedented new way. And so was born the Dulux Let's Colour Project—an open invitation to communities around the world to change gray spaces into colorful environments, done in collaboration with the people living in the neighborhoods themselves.

The very first iteration of the project started in 2010 with four cities in four different countries—the UK, India, Brazil, and France—where in conjunction with hundreds of volunteers (and 6,000 liters of paint), Dulux helped paint schools, streets, squares, and buildings.

Fernanda Romano, who was the creative director at Dulux's ad agency at the time, Euro RSCG, describes the process of how they came up with the idea. Passionate about her craft, Fernanda describes the process by which she got involved and how the project changed her life forever. She says, "The words 'Let's Colour' was the first thing I wrote, the day I came back from the pitch, and then I thought, *This is too obvious*, and I parked it. Then ten days before the final presentation, I went to the planner after we had been struggling for a while to encapsulate it, and he said [of 'Let's Colour'], 'Why did you put it away? That's perfect!'"

She continues, "The first thing we presented was a blog, because we wanted to start building a community. We added something crucial: participation. Because if people weren't part of it, they [would] have no ownership of it. So the painting events need[ed] to happen with the community. The brief was finding gray and dull spaces, historical city centers, schools, hospitals, parking lots, places where people come together . . . places that could use a bit of color. [We said,] 'We'll give you the paint, and teach you how to paint, but if you don't paint, there is no deal. And then we're going to document the painting events and turn that into a film, and use that as the invitation to the world.' And it all [came] together with 'Let's Colour' . . . [which] says, 'Come with me and let's do it together.' I get goose bumps just thinking about it."

Dulux turned the process into social media content and documentary films—and even into a two-minute TV spot—which were shared all around the world. The resulting film won a prestigious Ads Worth Spreading award from the TED organization. Hundreds more people started emailing and tweeting at the brand, asking how they could get involved—from everyday citizens in Italy, Chile, Indonesia, and other locations to the governor of Bangkok, who asked them to bring the project to his city.

More recently, Dulux started harnessing the power of pop culture by teaming up with artists and musicians to take the Let's Colour Project to a whole new artistic level. For instance, in the city of Marseille, France, the brand collaborated with mural artist Matt W. Moore, electronic musicians Monsieur Monsieur, and video directors Le Groupuscule to create an amazing video called *Walls are Dancing*. They transformed city walls with colorful, crazy geometric designs that were then animated into a music video—a gift to the people of Marseille.

Today Fernanda runs her own successful design and innovation firm, the Malagueta Group, which helps organizations like Johnson

& Johnson, ESPN, and Telefonica create disruptive change. When we ask Fernanda what made her the happiest about the Dulux experience, she doesn't even hesitate: "I think what I'm happiest about is that I allowed my work to change me," she says. "In India, I needed to help them because we were losing time, we were in a historic street in Rajasthan, and I was in the middle of the community, and it was so hot, and I took one of the rollers and started, and they came and hugged me and took pictures with me, and I really lived what I was telling other people to live. The paint fell on my head; I spent three hours in the shower, because otherwise I was going to have to shave my head. I have these Chuck Taylors that I wore to every event, and [they have] paint of all colors on them, and I still have them. . . . I was so proud that I wasn't bullshitting people; I was living what I was telling other people to do. I'm really proud of it; it really changed my life."

To date, Dulux has donated around 675,000 liters of paint to projects around the world, with hundreds of events worldwide, from China to Africa to South America and Europe. It has created a groundswell of positive support from citizens around the world.

It also addresses one of key examples of what is known as "cause-washing" or "purpose-washing": touting a noble cause without following through with authenticity. When a company spends $100,000 doing something good but spends $10 million advertising that project, that comes across as fake and inauthentic—advertising masquerading as social good. But if you leave a legacy of a street made beautiful, the positive impact lasts for far longer than an ephemeral TV commercial. It's ROP not ROI: "return on purpose" not "return on investment". As Fernanda says, "Your ad is a beautiful street; your out-of-home was the amazing facade of a museum."

WHY WE LOVE THIS EXAMPLE: Instead of adding to the noise and clutter of people's daily lives by putting up advertising billboards everywhere, Dulux listened to what communities were asking for—a way to brighten up their schools and playgrounds and community centers. And by treating them as involved citizens, not just consumers, Dulux created an army of participants and advocates for the brand. A simple, scalable, colorful idea that could translate to any country around the world.

Ahmen

Chief Development Officer, Sheltering Arms and Hip-Hop Artist

Movements that drive change—whether for market conditions or social conditions—are powered by citizens using their voices and actions to shake the status quo; or as Ahmen proudly calls them, "Troublemakers." As a nonprofit leader by day and hip-hop artist by night, Ahmen is on a mission to inspire artists to take a social stance in their work—and nonprofits to take a more "cultural entrepreneurship" approach in theirs, to inspire more citizens to create an even playing field for all.

It is a packed house in the Hippodrome Theatre, on the campus of the University of Florida. However, on this day, instead of an energetic crowd of college kids, the room is filled with excited change makers and movement builders in the field of public-interest communications, convened for the *frank*2016 gathering. Ahmen, a hip-hop artist and self-professed Troublemaker is about to take the stage. An event for public-interest professionals is not exactly where you expect to see a rapper, but Ahmen is no average rapper; that is only half his persona. His other half is an executive at a leading nonprofit, and he is there as part of a bigger mission—to inspire artists to take a social stance in their work and nonprofits to take a more cultural entrepreneurship approach in theirs.

A few months later, we meet Ahmen (real name Mohan Sivaloganathan) at a Manhattan restaurant and bar, tucked quietly in the otherwise hectic streets of midtown New York. He is tall, slim, smartly dressed, with a clean-shaven head. Although he is the self-proclaimed Batman of social impact, during the lunch hours of this spring day, he is looking every bit the part of the alter ego Bruce Wayne.

Ahmen's day job is as the chief development officer and senior vice president of Sheltering Arms, where he leads the fund-raising and revenue-generating efforts. Sheltering Arms is a nonprofit whose mission is to strengthen the education, well-being, and development of vulnerable children, youth, and families across the New York metro area.

Ahmen's path to this role was far from an expected one. He started as a brand marketer at Procter & Gamble, during a time in his life when he was becoming increasingly conscious of institutionalized systems in education and economics that were creating what he calls "uneven playing fields" in America and internationally. He began to ask himself, "Am I on the right side of this or the wrong side? And what can I do about it?"

Inspired to act, Ahmen left Procter & Gamble and went to work as a marketing director at the nonprofit Teach for America. However, Ahmen realized that as transformative as his work there could be, he was only scratching the surface of the number of people he could reach and the number of ways he could positively affect the world.

He says, "[I asked myself], 'How can I really exert my voice? How can I really extend my message and be able to cover even more people?' And that brought me to the passion of hip-hop music, which has always been the voice for communities, for generations, for billions of people. It was a voice for me growing up. I [decided I] need to commit to [it] too. I [couldn't] just commit to an area of passion at one part of my life; I [had] to commit all in. So then I decided that my Bruce Wayne side [was] going to be where I [would do] this executional work [at Teach for America] during the day, and my Dark Knight side of me [could] be hip-hop and could be when I use my voice to really get the attention of legions of people and be able to drive catalytic change at a much broader level. So I think coming from that point of reminding me why I made that decision to go to Teach for America, committing to my why has taken me on a pretty exciting journey."

We asked Ahmen how he would define his why. He says, "My why is my belief in people and what people can do. I believe that positive change is possible. I've seen so much change that has happened in the world since I've being doing this work over the past decade now. I've seen incredible reforms in juvenile justice that people would never have thought to be possible. I talked with people who, after seeing some of my shows and hearing my message in my songs about social change and the impact that we can have . . . literally have tears rolling down their cheeks because they feel like my music resonates so much with them."

He continues, "One of my favorite quotes from Martin Luther

King Jr. is 'the fierce urgency of now.' And that's pretty much how I operate my life now. We can't afford to wait. I have this urgency in every moment because I feel that sense of frustration in what's happening to the world; I feel that sense of potential. I have a feeling of obligation in what I need to be doing, and I know what can happen positively if we take the right action and if we unite with one another and actually try to advance important social causes and personal causes, and I also know what can happen if we don't, which means we perpetuate things in a status quo we've been unhappy with for generations now. That is why I'm fully committed to being the Batman of social impact, being a Troublemaker. There is no exception to that now; that is who I am 100 percent."

Ahmen's deep passion and energy for this Troublemaker movement—citizens using their voices and action to shake the status quo—is contagious. It's clear that these alter egos within him are creating a compelling whole to his being and role in the world. We speak about the notion of art and social impact fitting together, and he has an interesting take. "We received an article a while back comparing cultural entrepreneurship to social entrepreneurship, and [it] said that social entrepreneurship is in many ways the new specific tangible innovations that are being created to deliver change from a social standpoint. And the cultural entrepreneurship is the beliefs, the mind-sets, cultures, and values that are the underpinnings for social entrepreneurship. I think you need that fundamental set of beliefs so that we can be creators of a better world."

As cultural entrepreneurs, Ahmen believes artists should play an important role in creating a better world, and that they can do so by speaking to the hearts and minds of their fans, not just as consumers of their art but also as responsible citizens in our world. He says, "I think artists have an absolute obligation to have some sort of a role here, because the thing is, they're beneficiaries of the social contract. You don't just become famous by yourself and [with] nobody supporting you. Now, if you're an artist, then people are buying your album. And you gotta have some sort of thought of what [they are] dealing with in their lives. Now, does that mean that you need to go out and fund like millions and millions of dollars in, like, cancer research? No, it doesn't mean that. But it does mean that you should respect the role that you have to play within the global environment."

He continues, "I think that far too often artists will feel like, 'I'm just going to do my own thing.' You know, 'I'm not going to try to change the world.' A lot of them excuse themselves. Like, 'I'm not trying to change the world, I'm just trying to be an artist.' Well, why not? That's what I always say to myself: 'Why can't I try to do that?' We need to be able to look in the mirror and say, 'Things could be a little bit better, and I've got this platform to be able to accelerate that type of change. We can make change happen.'"

Specifically, Ahmen thinks celebrities and nonprofits should create more win-win relationships. "I think that celebrities have a certain platform and access that most nonprofits are not going to have," he says. "The critical part of it is to ensure that it's a two-way handshake that happens. I think what happens way too much right now is nonprofits are essentially beholden to celebrities that they are lucky enough to be able to engage; you know, they want to get paid a fee, and then that person is gone. I mean, there [are] so many problems with that. For one, you gotta have nonprofits spend so much to get somebody to support them, which is ridiculous, right? You're already cash-strapped to begin with.

"That's a completely unleveled playing field. So I think nonprofits have to come to the table and make sure that this is a mutual win-win what's happening here. So if it's a celebrity and you can say, 'No, you're not going to come to our event just one time and then that's it. You're going to donate or you're going to volunteer on an ongoing basis or you're going to spread the word for us or you're going to do mentoring, coaching.' [There are] so many different ways to get involved. But I think we really need to shift the way that things are being done and build much more respect for the social sector because people are seeing just how important it can be in everybody's everyday life, not just for those Mother Teresas who are out there doing great work."

Ahmen continues, "Increasingly, younger generations are seeing brands and individuals that impact our society in positive ways as more appealing to them. And because nonprofits are essentially in the business of doing that every day, there is a certain benefit, almost kind of a halo effect, [that] a nonprofit partnership can provide to a celebrity or brand. The big opportunity for nonprofits today is to recognize and leverage this moment in time to reposition themselves as valuable partners for brands and celebrities that want to impact society in meaningful ways."

Ahmen believes the key is for nonprofits to be better and more audacious storytellers of their work and the impact it can have on the world. He says, "You know, I will give you a specific example [from Sheltering Arms]. They've been around for a long time, and we had this brand that was somewhat antiquated, very conservative, working in the social services field doing really good work. But not many people knew about it then, and that was kind of the nature of the sector: 'Here, you do what you do, and you serve people really well, and that's it.' Then we realized that wasn't going to accelerate for us, it wasn't going to create the kind of partnership that we are discussing here. You need to be able to pull people with it. So at that moment we needed to describe what [it is] that we stand for.

"So what we said is, 'What we stand for is a compassionate, innovative organization that transforms the lives of local New Yorkers, and in doing that work, we are a go-to leader for change.' So, that's what we wanted to be. That's where we felt like we were at our best, and that's what we thought we [could] grow into. Now fast-forward to a year later: We've gone into this full comprehensive rebrand, and we've been able to attract celebrity ambassadors through the galas for two years in a row for the first time ever. We've never been able to do that. We've been able to attract corporate honorees for the first time; we have dramatically increased [the] number of corporate partnerships we [have]. We have volunteers from corporations who are coming to us now. We actually used to reach out to corporations all the time to try to start partnerships; we don't even do that now. Now they are coming to us. We have board members coming to us knocking on our doors; they want to be able to get involved. Our recruitment efforts for staff are much stronger than ever before. I think that happens when people don't just see the good work that you're doing but they see what you stand for and the major form of change that you represent."

It's clear from the energy in Ahmen's voice that seeing people "get it" is invigorating. He shares those moments when his message, whether delivered as an NGO executive or as a hip-hop artist, really touches people. "What makes me happy, what makes me proudest are the moments that violate people's schema, the moments where somebody thought that the system was supposed to operate a certain way, that things were supposed to happen in a certain way, and we were able to completely change that," he says. "So for an example, from a music standpoint . . . I talk with people who literally tell me, 'Hey, man, I saw you on that stage and I thought you were some sort of math nerd; you [look] like an IT guy or something like that. Man, I never thought you'd be able to flow like that. Like, that music . . . wasn't the type of music I expected to be coming from you. And it's real. And where can I find it, and where can I download it?' You know, like they didn't see that coming. They didn't expect that at all, you know?"

Ahmen also speaks of his recent experience at the *frank2016* conference, saying, "At a recent conference of forward-thinking leaders, I debuted 'Our Time,' the debut single from my new album.

The response convinced me that this album is the catalyst that we need in this moment. One person came to me with tears trickling down her cheeks and telling me she felt the urgency of this moment like never before.

"When it comes to my day job, so to speak, when I talk with people who used to think that kids in [the] South Bronx . . . [are] drug dealers, that they are violent, they're in gangs, they have no hope, and they have no future. And then they find out actually they have the same work ethic that you and I do, maybe even more work ethic, and . . . when you give them an opportunity to succeed, they'll go out and do an incredible job in the work that they have. In the schooling opportunity that they have, they can go out and do really incredible things."

Ahmen continues, "You know, we had a kid in our foster care program that actually went to the White House and presented at the [annual White House] Science Fair. You know, this is in foster care! Fifty percent of the kids who age out of foster care wind up homeless or in public support by the time they are age twenty-five. You know people don't see that coming, right? That's not where these schemas are oriented to. So those moments where we violated these schemas, that's when I know we've had their attention; and now that I've got your attention, now let's see where we can go from here. You know, those are the things that really make me really proud, because I know that it's going to stick around and last for a long time."

Seeing the impact of his work and art continues to fuel Ahmen's drive. He speaks about the next phase in this work. "My plan is very much for the Troublemaker Movement that I've been promoting now for the past couple of years. So with that, [I am] working on a new album that . . . I am hoping . . . can serve as sort of this rallying call, this torch for people. Give them a voice, give them a soundtrack that will be able to push them forward as Troublemakers, and with that, what I am also trying to do is build as many partnerships as possible.

"I want to be able to do a partnership so we can actually be able to execute; that would not be only promoting the idea for being a Troublemaker but actually doing 'It.' So for instance, I'm going to be performing in a show with Fusion to be protesting solitary confinement. So those are the types of things I'm excited about doing. A specific cause I really care about with an organization that I know is committed and still wants to make a difference. I'm trying to find these different brands and nonprofit community organizations [that] are out there [and] share this belief in what I am doing and are doing great work. [And I wan t to know] how [I can] uniquely add to that as a hip-hop artist, as a nonprofit leader, and be able to support the incredible things that they do. Those are like the two big elements that I am going to be pushing forward that will hopefully be able to build steam and build more momentum for the Troublemaker Movement and turn it into something that can globally accept people."

WHY WE LOVE THIS EXAMPLE: We love this story because it truly captures the power of connecting with people as citizens and creating offerings and messages that feed the good in them and inspire them to take action. How Ahmen combines the two sides of his personality—the social entrepreneur and the artist—provides an inspiring example of how to live an integrated life of purpose.

Aerosyn-Lex Mestrovic

Artist

Artists play a powerful role in shaping the way we see ourselves, each other, and the world around us. One artist who understands the responsibility of that power is Aerosyn-Lex Mestrovic, who shares how brands, "the new patron saints," afford him the opportunity to make the world a gallery for his art and inspire other young artists to use their talents and voices for good.

Watching a video of the artist Aerosyn-Lex Mestrovic, more commonly known as Lex, create what he calls "Living Paintings" is a mesmerizing experience. You can see these beautiful and vivid colors mix and wash over a canvas in ways that are both free-flowing and controlled by an invisible hand. It gives the viewer an immersive experience in how his work is created, without ever actually seeing him in the process. It captures the wide range of motions that are required to make a single piece of his art. As Mastrovic described for CNN.com's monthly "The Art of Movement" coverage, "A living painting is many things. It's a painting process, it's a work of film, and it's an actual tactile painting."[2]

It is also a metaphor for his journey as an artist, a constant work in progress that is evolving in remarkable ways right before our eyes. Like his paintings, Lex has mixed a wide range of experiences and influences together in ways that were both intentional and beyond his control to become an award-winning designer, filmmaker, calligrapher, and creative director of the New York- and London-based record label Earnest Endeavours.

His impressive list of collaborators includes Kanye West, art icon Jeff Koons, acclaimed designers Dao-Yi Chow and Maxwell Osborne of Public School, and the legendary Parisian fashion house KENZO. He has become one of the most awarded artists in the contemporary art world, and beyond the art community, brands such as Nike, Beck's, Hennessy, and Dell have also taken notice, collaborating with him on a wide range of products and packaging.

However, his next body of work will likely be his most important. Lex shares how he partners with brands as "the new patrons" who afford him the opportunity to inspire other young artists around the world to affect the greater good.

---

2 Earl Nurse and Phoebe Parke. "Artist Creates 'Living Paintings' That Grow Before Your Eyes." CNN. 2014. http://www.cnn.com/2014/11/11/world/living-paintings-aerosyn-lex-mestrovic/index.html.

We meet in a Chelsea coffee shop. Dressed in his trademark black from head to toe, Lex has just returned from a two-week exhibit in Tokyo. Art from an early age has always seemed to be part of his life and identity. He tells us, "I think for me it's always been a pretty clear purpose. I don't remember really a time where I wasn't trying to be [an artist]. I mean, like, just as a kid I was drawing, painting, always doing the creative stuff, always interested and curious. And throughout school that was always what the teachers picked up on, they told my parents. My parents were supportive, so that idea [of] creativity was always a part of me.

"The idea to be creative—an artist, so to speak—that's always been the intent. How to manifest that, how to apply that, how to make a living from that, how to create a life from that, that's the harder aspect. That's the biggest challenge."

To Lex, a support structure can make all the difference in the world for whether or not artists can develop their crafts, particularly at a time when support for working artists seems to be diminishing every day. He says, "There's a saying that 'Art is for the eternally destitute or the inherently wealthy,' which means you're either the proverbial starving artist or you're somebody with a bankroll that can afford to do just whatever they want creatively. And so either it clicks or it doesn't, but it doesn't really matter. It is very little in between. There are statistically very few folks that as artists are able to, let's say, make a middle-class income. Those persons that are creative and artistic but want the security like to fall into creative industries where they work at an ad agency. They are designers, they are architects, they are creative professionals; but for fine artists, it's a very polarizing profession.

"The idea of how we define artists is changing because an artist is now devoid of the traditional infrastructure and support systems of endowments, of institutional framework, of residency programs, all that stuff. There's no longer really governmental institutional support for fine artists. You know, you have a lack of subsidies in New York, [where] there's no affordable space for artists. All the artists are driven out to second- or third tier-markets like Detroit, or wherever they can afford space to work. It's like impossible to do it."

This void is creating a clear and valuable role for brands, which are providing artists with resources and opportunities to expand the reach of their work. Interestingly, Lex believes brands are key for artists today because they can financially support their ability to create the art they want. He says, "So one way that artists are figuring how to do that is to collaborate with brands because brands are the new patron saints these days. You know, in the Renaissance you had the Catholic Church, you had the Medici family, you had these institutions that paid for Michelangelo to sculpt David or paint the Sistine Chapel. You know, these great masterworks [were] supported by patrons; that's few and far between now. We have Red Bull, we got Nike, we got Scion, we got AXE, we got Bombay Sapphire, all these companies that are seeing the cultural value of what art is, which is always an indicator of the cultural temperament of that time. And I think brands in the [United] States and Europe, more so than Asia, are learning to coexist rather than co-opt creative content."

Lex believes this recent explosion in popularity of partnerships between brands and artists is part of a convergence that has been in the making for decades. As brands become more essential as financial supporters of the art community, these partnerships are becoming more common and acceptable in the art world. But that doesn't mean artists don't struggle to find the balance between their creative desires and commercial demands.

Lex says, "The idea of art and commerce together, you know, it's not something that's new. There's precedent there. You've had Jeff Koons do H&M; before that you had Schiaparelli using Salvador Dali for scarves, you had Yves Saint Laurent using Piet Mondrian. These things have happened for decades. I think it's becoming viable and it's no longer as stigmatizing for an artist to do something commercially and then have a gallery to show and sell to collectors."

But, Lex acknowledges there is still a paradox that exists for him as well. "There's still a disconnect, but for me it's a crux because I'm struggling to find that balance myself; that's my conversation every day," he says. "It's like, all right, you know, I'm making my money with these collaborations. Money is great! I don't want to be a starving artist, I'm trying to live in Chelsea and have a dope studio, and I like to wear shiny shoes, you know, have a leather jacket. But I also want to make real, serious, conceptual work, which I do, but I want to make the work that I want to make. But I also like the certain quality of life so, you know, I'm able to make money on these collaborations. I also am super-inspired by the collaborations! It's like if I have the opportunity to create women's clothing for a Japanese market, that's like a great opportunity, you know. I'm as excited about doing that as I would be about making a new painting."

He continues, "I like that idea of that balance. I hope that any project that I do, whether it's going to be on sale at Target or on a white wall in a gallery, there's the same level of intent, the same level of, hopefully, emotion or commitment to that process. When you're an artist, the gallery is your gallery; the white wall the cubicle you know that system or framework is your gallery. When you create products, the world is your gallery. You can have somebody wear your artwork, somebody could buy a table that you designed and craft it and it lives with them for decades; that's an interesting and rewarding thing for me."

In recent years, Lex has indeed made the world his canvas, creating groundbreaking works across fine art, fashion, technology, and product collaboration. Lex tells us why the ability to create without limits is so exciting to him, saying, "You know, it's a great challenge being a curious, inquisitive, inspired person. When you get that challenge, the gears start turning. What would I do?"

Lex discusses the details of an upcoming project in partnership with the perfume house Sixth Sense. "It's a series of nine different fragrances," he says. "I do all the art, where each fragrance is based on a poisonous flower. Now you start learning about how fragrance affects the brain and creates the most amount of, like, semantic connections, and the brain's chemistry to create vivid memories from fragrance, and then you start thinking about the stories you can tell with that, how that interfaces with all the other stuff . . . like, that's great. I've never done that . . . We just debuted in Paris fashion week. Yeah, pretty excited. Stoked!"

With all the cool projects Lex continues to create and share with the world, he is also very conscious of the power and opportunity for artists to influence a greater good. He says, "I think what's interesting, as an artist you have a wide ability to leverage a voice. And so, you know, artists have always been bellwethers for society. They've always been at the vanguard of social or political topics. They've always been kind of griots, persons kind of illuminating aspects of our society whether it be through movements of abstractionism in reference to talking about art itself, or stuff that's more politically geared. Whatever it might be, artists always have had a very specific space in terms of their voice and impact, and I think for me the ability to apply that craft hopefully in some way [is important], you know, [to] leave a legacy of work that is not only connected to the time in which it was created but hopefully indicative of something larger. Hopefully, the work that I do can be seen years from now and something might be garnered from that."

Beyond the work, Lex is increasingly inspired to create a legacy and larger impact through educating the next generation of young artists on how to use their voices, and through using his art to connect people around the world across lines of difference. Lex shares an encounter that made a transformative impact on his life, helping him to recognize his power to create change.

ARTISTS

HAVE ALWAYS BEEN

BELLWETHERS

FOR SOCIETY

AEROSYN-LEX
MESTROVIC

It started with an invitation from his friend, Ford model Monica Watkins, who created the nonprofit Art in Motion (AIM), whose mission is to inspire, uplift, and strengthen local communities by cultivating their children through the arts. According to its website, AIM has created art, music, fashion, filmmaking, and photography workshops for more than 1,300 children in Hong Kong, Cambodia, Haiti, the Dominican Republic, France, and the United States, and helped to facilitate donations of more than 2,000 pounds of art supplies for underserved communities worldwide. Empowering the future, many AIM youth have gone on to become filmmakers, professional artists, and professional musicians. Many have come back to donate their time to travel with AIM on their teaching expeditions.

Lex says, "So there was . . . a program based in New York and Hong Kong that was headed up by this wonderful girl, Monica Watkins, model and activist, and she partnered with a program called HandsOn Hong Kong which is like a big government program there. I didn't know what I was getting into, and she asked me, 'Do you want to come to Hong Kong for, like, two weeks and teach?' and I'm like, 'All right.' And then when I got there, it was like a really great experience. Art in motion's idea is art as a platform for education for underprivileged kids, first in New York, [and] then [it] ended up in Haiti, Africa, [the] Caribbean. So they do a lot of work.

"And they partnered with [HandsOn Hong Kong] to teach underprivileged kids in Hong Kong. People are like, 'Oh, Hong Kong; it's full of rich finance people.' But you know, there are still a lot of migrant workers that come from Mainland China, Southeast Asia, to find work. Kids are orphaned or they don't have a home. There was a group of thirty-some-odd kids ranging from four to sixteen. Most of them were girls, and some of them were sexually trafficked as teenagers. It's crazy stuff, but then you would never guess it talking to them. Some of the kids had lost their parents; some are orphans."

He continues, "And there's the language barrier. But utilizing this kind of universal language of art and creativity, we had all these activities. [Monica Watkins] brought out stylists, designers, fashion designers, photographers, and videographers and created this whole [event] to show them the creative process. Essentially we were recreating a photo shoot and art show, utilizing the creativity of the kids. We were telling the story, 'Hey, we are going to give you guys the tools, and then we are going to make you guys front and center. You're the star of this show'—which was a fund-raiser at the Ritz-Carlton. I think we raised over $100,000 for this program. And it was all about empowering the kids to do their thing; they were the girls who got their hair and makeup done, and they walked on a runway; they wore their own clothing that we designed with them, and so it was about facilitating that creativity, showing them what's possible, letting them do it like they were the stars. It was a really impactful moment."

Lex reflects on his own childhood. He was a child drawn to art but who was not given a blueprint on how to use it. "Whatever I liked [as a kid], I did it because I just wanted to figure out how to do it, and I did it for myself. I never really knew that, 'Oh, this is something that people do and make a living out of it.' If I would have known that, I would've been much more informed at an earlier age to maybe have wasted a little less time or, you know, taken more of a direct route. So that's, I think, a valuable thing: setting a good example."

The experience continues to affect and inspire him as an artist. "I always said that when you volunteer, you think you're doing something very selfless. But it ends up being very selfish because you gain so much more out of it than you put in. I believe in the stuff I do, but then when you do it for like a generation of folks or like somebody that's coming up, you really feel it in a different way. And then that's a rewarding feeling. And sometimes you're just focused on the bottom line or like a good activation or a dope party, and then you get through it and enjoy it, and then you're like, 'All right, next thing.' But you get a lot out of it. That's partly where I'm at now—I'm interested in pursuing the educational aspect of it. One hundred percent, Art in Motion helped ignite that, and so now I'm like, 'Yeah, let's figure out how to do [more of] that.'"

As part of that effort to do more, Lex is now working with the US-Japan Leadership Program, where he says he is "looking to develop some educational programs highlighting the creative relationships that exist between the US and Japan."

So for Lex—a creative and curious kid from Buenos Aires who grew up drawing and painting for fun—the journey is coming full circle. Now as an accomplished artist, with the world as his gallery, Lex is helping young people see the power and possibilities their own creativity can offer. As he speaks about these opportunities to use his talents to facilitate a greater good, it's wonderful to see his renewed sense of purpose and excitement for his work and future.

He says, "So what's interesting is, again, having put in the years of work, like, to just do cool stuff, now it's like, 'All right, well, now I could do *good* cool stuff.' You know, let's use the relationships that we have for a greater good than just, like, selling shoes or something. That's what's interesting. And I hope [for that] to be part of all the stuff that I do going forward. Not every project, but moving forward—if that's a part of my story for the next few decades—and again there's something that's for the greater good, that would be really rewarding. I love doing it."

WHY WE LOVE THIS EXAMPLE: It reminds us that despite the decreasing institutional support afforded to them, artists continue to have a very specific and essential space in our world, in terms of their voice and impact. Artists are often our conscience, pointing out where and how we can do better. They have the ability to reshape how we see ourselves and our relationship with the world around us. And now, as we live in a time where the problems and possibilities in our world are more evident than ever before, it just may be that the most powerful thing artists can do is to help unleash the moral imaginations of the next generation of young artists, and inspire them to see the whole world as a canvas for creating a better picture of humanity.

4.
LEAD WITH THE COOL, BUT BAKE IN THE GOOD

Today it is no longer enough for a brand just to be "Good"; it must also be "Cool." A new generation of customers is demanding more social consciousness from the brands it buys; but it also wants to make sure that social consciousness is balanced out by the right design, the right aesthetic, the right story told in an authentic and meaningful way.

In this section, we meet Jason Mayden, a former head of design for Nike who is now at Accel Partners in Silicon Valley, and talk to him about how designers have a golden opportunity to design not just products but organizations in a way that is diverse and cool. We meet the multitalented Mimi Valdés, the chief creative officer for superstar Pharrell's i am OTHER, who talks about how she's using her skills as a storyteller to make the world a more positive, inclusive place. And then we meet Jocelyn Cooper, the cofounder of the music festival and cultural platform Afropunk and talk to her about how she's creating a movement that reflects the new America—more racially, sexually, and gender diverse than ever before.

Jason Mayden

Designer, Accel Partners; Cofounder, Slyce.io

Jason Mayden is a designer on a mission. In Silicon Valley, a space renowned for innovation and entrepreneurship, Jason is looking to disrupt the Valley's homogenous status quo by applying his exceptional design talents beyond just physical products, to more boldly apply them to culture—the "first product of any organization"—and in the process make organizations more inclusive, diverse, and accessible to talent previously ignored and undervalued by the tech world.

Before making the move to Silicon Valley, Jason was widely respected among sneaker enthusiasts for his stellar design work with the culturally iconic Nike and Jordan brands. We first were introduced to Jason's story by listening to him speak to a room filled with aspiring footwear designers in Los Angeles at an event hosted by career curriculum platform Behind the Hustle. What struck us most while listening to Jason was his generosity of knowledge and spirit. Although he could have easily played the role of the ultimate cool kid every sneakerhead in the room wanted to be around, he instead shared his experiences with humility and a sincere desire to help each of them create a path to success in business.

Positioned in the front of the room, he stands more than six feet tall, with brown skin, a big smile, and, as he jokes, a perfect round head for the bald look that he pulls off almost as well as his former boss Michael Jordan. He shares his journey of growing up as a kid from the Southside of Chicago drawing sketches of Jordan sneakers for fun to realizing his dream of working for Jordan as the brand's first intern, ultimately becoming its senior global design director. Jason talks about how, after thirteen years of designing some of Nike's biggest successes—including overseeing Nike's digital platform, Nike+—he left Nike to take on a new opportunity: helping people reach an optimal level of well-being as the vice president of design at Vessyl, an intelligent cup that knows and automatically records the calories, sugar, and protein you consume in liquid form and sends it to your mobile device for tracking.

His stories and advice at the Behind the Hustle event were real, relatable, and moving; and it was clear that his presence that day and the work he chooses to do are all part of a greater calling. Vessyl, a product with a focus on helping people live healthier lives, was particularly personal to Jason. He tells a story in an interview with Fast Company of experiencing a distressing moment of hearing his son tell him "I do not love who I am" while struggling with weight gain (which was later diagnosed by doctors as the result of a collection of food allergies).

Upon seeing the challenges his son was facing, Jason took a break from his job to focus on the health of his son, which he described as "the natural choice that any father would make."

Months later, Jason says he received a text message from the vice president of Mark One, telling him they were working on the Vessyl product. Jason says, "I took that as a sign."

A little more than a year after first hearing him speak at the Behind the Hustle event, we were introduced to Jason by the event's founder, Kenny Mac. We sat down to talk with Jason to hear what he was up to. Passionate and purposeful, he speaks of his new roles with the clarity and energy of someone who once boldly proclaimed he wants to "be faster than the future."

Jason tells us, "I have three jobs. At Accel Partners [a venture capital firm] I help to amplify and deepen the value and overall impact of design of things within companies, whether they are in the early stage or growth stage of companies. At Stanford [as a media designer/lecturer at the Hasso Plattner Institute of Design], I help to create moments of critical discourse that allow for true cultural exchange, with the sole intent of providing exposure for these students that are often forgotten about. My company [Slyce.io] that I cofounded with Bryant Barr and NBA superstar Steph Curry is about creating a more efficient, more deliberate, more consistent workflow between brands and influencers, to get the most value from their moment of being in the spotlight."

He speaks about the common thread between these ventures and why they are so aligned with his sense of purpose in this moment in time. "The thing that ties all three of them together is this mind-set that what I do is not about me. What I do is to serve other people, using my gifts and talents to help them get the most out of their opportunity. I feel like God has designed me for many things at different times. In this season of my life, my 'why' is to be a counter-narrative to what people think is accessible, in the tech industry and the other industries I am in, education and entrepreneurship."

Silicon Valley's problems with lack of diversity in ethnicity and gender have been well-documented. Jason strongly believes diversity, inclusion, and exposure—in all forms—lead to greater innovation and better entrepreneurs and founders. As a result, he is looking to help create more inclusive organizational cultures in which all people feel free to be their most authentic selves.

"You know a lot of my contemporaries go through this very interesting experience of what I call 'cultural sanitization,' where they want to be included so much in the masses that they are willing to forfeit the very thing that makes them unique and desirable in the first place," Jason says. "My mission is to be myself authentically and hopefully inspire other people to find their own voice and create their own language that defines them, and not join someone else's lane.

"I like to tell people that the mind-set of an innovator is to solve the biggest problem that helps the most people. The biggest problem is that we put up barriers as to what we think is cool or as to what we think is smart or intelligent or valuable. And I just want to stand in opposition [to that] and just be myself. Unapologetically be myself and say: 'If you don't think I'm cool or worthy, that's okay. That's your opinion. But I feel like there is a lane of people that will appreciate my perspective and will find courage and strength in me standing against trying to fit in. Because I don't want to fit in if, to fit in, I have to forfeit who I am.' I was just raised to believe that you can play the game, but you don't have to play yourself."

Jason believes part of the problem is the narrow images people associate with designers that leave many talented people feeling like outsiders. He says, "This may sound very controversial, but I would like to see the archetype of design not be a white British male. That, to me, is a falsehood. When I go to look at anything that is design driven, there is usually a white male with a British accent or a derivative of a British accent. While that's cool, I think that's also very defeating for anyone that's a minority, because it's like, 'I don't sound like Jony Ive, or if I don't look like the founder of Dyson vacuum[s], or if I don't look like Marc Newson. But if I don't look or feel like these people how do I find a job that will think I am valuable?'"

He continues, "That to me is the image that we celebrate, and for design, it is very limiting; it's very Eurocentric, and it's usually the same types of people. And I think that's very hurtful for our industry, because we're supposed to be the industry of inclusiveness; we're the equivalent of sports. Where if you have the talent, if you do real work, you should be able to succeed by designing. It's a meritocracy. It should be about the work. Not about the accent, not about the pedigree, just about the work—because it really comes down to that issue.

"But yet we're still struggling with the archetypal images that are put out there, stating [that if] you're not of European descent and not, you know, you don't wear all black, you don't attend fashion week, you don't have an accent, [then] you're not a designer. But I think that is an absolute lie. Because to say that eliminates every single culture that has contributed to what we now call design, particularly the African culture that has created more things than any other culture on this planet, because of our historical advantage. And then second to the African culture . . . is the Asian culture, and their contributions. It's fascinating to see how very deliberately our industry has only celebrated European contributions in art and design, when a lot of these concepts are borrowed or literally taken from other cultures.

"So I think that's the big shift: celebrating the contributions from all people to the creative arts, not just some people. Because I see so many students that say they've never met a black designer, and

I'm like, 'Half the stuff you're wearing is made by black designers.' So half the stuff you read or all these examples or technology to be used—there's some person of color that has been involved. But the outer perception is that we are nowhere to be found.

"In the culture that I live in now, which is an achievement culture, a culture of collective courage, certain people are inspired to speak up and others are told to stick within this lane. Here I am carving out my own narrative, my own unique path, coming from a very different background.

"That gives me a little bit of confidence to speak up about what I believe is hurtful for innovation, which is the mind-set that we all have to be alike in order to succeed in this industry. I think that the moment I am in [Silicon] Valley, with the topic being about race and inclusion, for me, I think that my contribution in this conversation can go far beyond my skin color and my upbringing."

Jason believes the key is exposure. "You know a lot of what I do is behind the scenes. I am a big fan of exposure. A lot of people are fans of opportunity. But for the minority demographic that is being heavily targeted now by tech, they think the way you solve these issues is to say, 'Hey, let's find talented people and give them jobs because they can't fend for themselves and we have to feed them.' I don't believe that to be true. What they need is the exposure and understanding and a lot of times acknowledgment that they are doing a lot of what is being done here [in Silicon Valley], but it's a different vocabulary.

"So what I try to do is to create these moments of exposure for young people of color, or for women or any other minority group, to realize that they already have what it takes to be here. They just don't have the vocabulary. No one's told them that if they are out in New York and they have their own small businesses and they are hustling handmade shirts that they are an entrepreneur. They just think they are hustling. But that's entrepreneurship, that's building a business, that is understanding consumer needs, that's demand planning, that's cost saving, that's inventory, that's accounting, that's brand management. It's everything you need to be a founder [of a company].

"But because we've allowed this generation to be conditioned to be consumers, now we are trying to undo that by . . . saying, 'You know what? We want to give you a job at our company. Because if you work at our company, now you're special.' But my mind-set [is], we need to give them the tools and the courage to start their own company, to start their own businesses, because in the future the problems are prevented because the founders are already embedded in the concepts of inclusion and diversity, because they come from diverse backgrounds."

Jason is creating opportunities for various communities to gain exposure to the inner workings of Silicon Valley. He speaks about the transformational affect it has on the young people in particular.

"As an example, I took about 110 young students from varying socioeconomic backgrounds—primarily African American and Latino—to Y Combinator, which is an accelerator here [in Silicon Valley] for start-ups. This is the first time this group of students, ranging from middle school to graduate school, [has] ever been in this place, [has] ever felt accepted in this place. And they heard for the first time that the vocabulary that they use is valuable to this industry.

"And just the mind-set shift in the room was amazing, because my whole thesis is around exposure shifts. Not internships, not access, just exposure. Just provide people with different examples of success and show them that it's possible, and they will step up to the plate, because people become what you expect of them. And right now, they set the expectation that 'minority' means 'needing a significant amount of training.' No, they don't. I mean, we know how to use technology because we consume most of it. We spend most of our money. We spend most of our time. We know how to use it. And we already know how to manipulate it to get the most out of it. But what we don't have is exposure to what it looks like on a daily basis on the creation side. We only have exposure to the consumption side."

Jason is very comfortable with his work mainly being behind the scenes. He is not doing this for attention or fame; rather he is driven by a deep commitment to expose diverse communities to the opportunities and resources that they need to be successful entrepreneurs.

"So every single thing that I do is not intended to make it to the media. It is intended to give the confidence and self-efficacy that is missing from this generation in minority talent. The ability to feel like they can do it and they have a safety net. Like most of the entrepreneurs who are successful, here are people who don't talk about it because they come from wealthy families and have a safety net. So they can take greater risks, but minorities, historically we only know risks. We only know sacrifice. We only know struggling. So we are predisposed to being great founders, because we have to live scrappy for generations. So the mind-set of being lean and being scrappy is not a unique concept to minorities. What is a new concept is the idea that that translates to being the founder of the company.

"So that's all . . . I'm trying to do: build a bridge back to where I've come from, the neighborhood I've come from, the mind-set that I used to have, [from] the mind-set and neighborhood that I'm living in now. And just tell them that, 'Yo, you can completely be yourself. Use all of the things that you've learned growing up in NY, Chicago, L.A., Houston, Medici, Tokyo, India to become something special and something that is real and authentic."

In these inner-city neighborhoods, Jason believes there is a wealth of untapped talent that can be the new founders of the next wave of successful companies. Talented, driven young people already equipped with the qualities venture capital firms like Accel are looking for but who lack the exposure Jason sees as essential. He describes this group in an essay he penned titled "The Rise of the Cultural Alchemist," a term he defines thus:

> "A 'Cultural Alchemist' can be defined as 14–25 years old, contextually educated, multiracial, methodically creative, socially aware, culturally blended and technologically proficient. They are driven by genuine interactions, exchanges of ideas, collective aspirations and access to experiences that lead to meaningful opportunities. They are not just looking for a job, they are looking for a mission and a purpose. They are the champions of the future.
>
> They do not believe in 'picking a lane.' They believe that they are the lane."

Jason is now "working to inspire and create access to opportunities for the emergent Cultural Alchemists of the world," who he believes "will define the way we live, work, play, interact, and dream."

As Jason continues to redesign organizational cultures in ways that enhance innovation and expand entrepreneurship, he thinks in the future, more designers will play driving roles in creating places where inclusiveness and exposure in all forms are leading to great design. He says, "You know, I think there will be more of a shift to designers who can become chief culture officers for companies. I think designers are going to radically change the way that human resource departments are created within the organization; if companies are forward-thinking and really understanding that the first product you create is your culture, and the first consumer is your employee base.

"I think that's how we're going to build better companies, better corporations, better governments, and better societies," Jason says. "By bringing the mind-set of human-centeredness into every discussion, not just when it comes to making a machine or making an app, but in building these organisms that we call organizations. So that, to me, is the future, and not like the distant future; it's in the next two, three years.

"Because when the millennials . . . you know, I'm at the beginning of the millennial era, where children born in the 1980s . . . there is no way that you can just throw money at us and keep us loyal. You have to be solving problems that we find interesting and relevant. You have to be a culture that is flexible and dynamic. You have to be willing to allow us to work in the way that we feel comfortable; meaning we may want to work from home, we may want to work on an airplane traveling somewhere, we may want to work at an office. But you have to be more fluid, not rigid. And those are all design problems, but design schools, they don't think about those jobs. So I would say that's what I'm seeing; that's what I am interested about. The further I get into this, in my current career, I feel like I am being pulled into being one of those people who helps create culture in companies. And it's fascinating, because I went to school to make product, and now I'm being asked to help create cultures, which is so interesting to see the shifts, you know."

WHY WE LOVE THIS EXAMPLE: We love the notion that culture is the most important product organizations create, that employees are the first customers, and that by designing inclusive cultures where employees are able to be and contribute their most authentic selves, you can bake in the "Good" in a powerful way.

The first product you create is your

culture,

and the first consumer is your

employee base.

Jason Mayden

Mimi Valdés

Chief Creative Officer, i am OTHER

i am OTHER, the creative umbrella for all of Pharrell Williams's ventures, knows exactly what it stands for: individuality, the uniqueness and diversity that makes us all valuable and beautiful. Mimi Valdés, its chief creative officer, shares how they embed that DNA in every story they tell across fashion, film, music, and beyond, to create a world where everyone sees the beauty in each OTHER.

It is a beautiful summer day, the kind of perfect weather you dream about during the long winter months. The energy seemingly everywhere in the city is vibrant and upbeat, making it almost impossible to have a bad day, even if you wanted to. A newly washed SUV drives through the busy traffic blasting the hit song "Happy" by Pharrell Williams, which feels like the perfect soundtrack for today's mood. Teens are outside, lined up on the sidewalk waiting to see the new coming-of-age film *Dope*.

The line of teens looks like a modern-day Benetton ad, where seemingly every possible ethnic group imaginable is represented and harmoniously interacting. They are all dressed in their freshest summer fashion; one kid has a hat nonchalantly turned backward as he tries his best to charm the petite Hispanic girl he has his sights on. His hat reads THE SAME IS LAME, and a quick glance at the line of footwear on display suggests that may be a mantra for this group. At least a dozen of the teens are in some different shade of a seemingly never-ending pantone of colored Adidas shell toes.

There is clearly a shared ethos among this group—individuality, creativity, coolness, and optimism—that connects them to each other and to a single brand, i am OTHER, which is the creator of the music in the streets, the clothing they are wearing from head to toe, and the movie they are waiting to see. We took a deeper look at i am OTHER and how the beauty of individuality is the purpose that links all their endeavors in fashion, film, and music.

i am OTHER is the umbrella brand for all the creative ventures for music superstar and cultural pied piper Pharrell Williams, and while every one of these cool kids knows Pharrell, it is Mimi Valdés, his creative partner and i am OTHER's chief creative officer who is a driving force in bringing this colorful, diverse world to life.

Summer days like this should feel familiar to Mimi, who grew up in New York, one of the most multicultural cities on the planet. She is used to seeing millions of people of every shade, gender, faith, and orientation, and knows each of them has a story to tell.

She is smart, confident, and connects with a genuine warmth and infectious youthful energy. As a journalist, she has told the stories of some of the biggest names in popular culture, and now as a chief creative officer, she is helping to inspire millions of others to celebrate their individuality through narratives across film, television, music, and products.

From a young age, Mimi was interested in learning about and telling stories, and so it makes sense that a natural storyteller born in the most eclectic city in the world would grow up to tell stories that capture and celebrate the unique diversity we all share. She says, "Being born and raised in New York City, in Manhattan, I went to school with everybody, right? When I walked down the street, I saw everybody. To me it is weird when you are in places where there aren't different kinds of people. So of course I have my eye out and heart in diversity, real diversity.

"I felt from a very young age that I was meant to tell stories. I was always attracted to it. I think in my head I am always first of all a journalist, always and forever, and I love good stories. I love stories that haven't been told before but yet are super relatable to people—just everyone, regardless of what your color, race, ethnicity, [or] sexual orientation is. Those are the kind of stories that I am always attracted to. I can't remember a moment of being like, 'OK, I want to tell stories,' but that was what I always felt like I was supposed to do, and then as time has gone on, it changes to different things. Right, it was working for magazines or websites or coming to work with Pharrell."

One of Mimi's first jobs after graduating from NYU was working at *Vibe*, an upstart magazine founded by Quincy Jones, which would grow to become one of the most authoritative and influential voices in youth culture. Starting as an intern, Mimi rose through the ranks to become editor in chief. She tells us, "When I became editor in chief of *Vibe*, I was the fourth or fifth one, and I remember thinking at the time—because I am a crazy Virgo that's always analyzing things—*OK, what's next after this? There is a possibility that this might not last forever.* But I wasn't sure what that [next step] would be, but I just remember thinking, *Just make sure you do a really, really good job. You have your relationships, and make sure that you cultivate them and cultivate them in a way that people aren't just dealing with you because you're the editor in chief of* Vibe."

Those Virgo instincts proved again to be valuable when *Vibe* was sold to a private equity company, which resulted in massive layoffs. Mimi says, "I remember when everything happened at *Vibe* I got phone calls from Jay Z and all these artists [who] reached out on some, like, 'Are you good? Are you OK?' [level]. And I remember saying, 'Aw, man! So people didn't deal with me just because I was editor in chief of *Vibe*. They honestly care about me, actually really are concerned that I am good.' And I felt proud about that, because I was like, *The important thing is, if you do a really good job, you'll figure it out.*

"So after that I went to *Latina* magazine, I was there for a while, became editor in chief there too. After that I was VP of digital content at BET.com."

Although the BET job didn't work out as she planned, it led her to i am OTHER with Pharrell, an opportunity that would unleash her creativity and purpose in ways beyond what she could have imagined. Given their friendship and kindred values, it was a perfect fit.

"Pharrell and I, you know, are friends for a reason; he is like my little brother," Mimi says. "We look at the world the same way, we share a lot of the same values and approaches to just life in general, so when it came time to start i am OTHER—he calls it a creative collective, and it's really the umbrella company for all of his ventures—he was just like, 'Come on board.' So I decided to quit."

Together, they began building the brand the way these authors believe all successful brands should be built: by starting with a clear understanding of what you stand for and the impact you want to make in the world. That collaborative process began with looking back at the core values that inspired Pharrell's music production and recording collaboration N*E*R*D, and identifying the core values they felt needed to be embedded in i am OTHER.

Mimi says, "The thing we thought about—just like what he did when he first came out with N*E*R*D—the reason why he made it, he wanted to somehow make being a nerd cooler, education cooler, being smart cool; that was the goal. So much so that when Shepard Fairey, who designed the HOPE poster for Obama, designed that N*E*R*D logo, the brain, it came from him being like, 'The brain represents education.' He's always wanted to promote that, and when it came time for i am OTHER, it was those same values. I always believed individuality is something that people should be proud of."

She continues, "And OTHER—the name of the company—actually came from Lauryn Hill, strangely enough. Years ago, when [Pharrell] was about to work for her, she told him, "I like what you guys do. You're different; but when you work with me, I need other,' and Pharrell was like, 'Oh my God! Other!' That always [stuck] in his head, so when it came time to revamp his company and he wanted a fresh start to look at stuff, the idea of otherness, that stood [out] in his head."

Whereas most brands bury their values and purpose in HR folders or on plaques in the corporate hallways, i am OTHER made it a point to proclaim theirs for the world to see, giving everyone a clear understanding of what they stand for and the principles that guide their community and everything they create. For example, Mimi says, "On the website, there's a manifesto of what 'other' is, and the importance of individuality and experiences being the new wealth. That came from wanting to explain the mentality, what it is and how we approach every project. So it's like everything is part of wanting to spread that idea of why individuality is a cool thing. Obviously, the world has changed, but we still have numbers of people being attacked or shunned or something because they are different. And we're like, 'Man, you are crazy. You are looking at the world in really not the right way,' because the beauty of this world is the fact that we are so different and we have different experiences and different lives, but at the same time there is a commonality and a desire to just do good and do good work that feels good.

Mimi shares how the importance of individuality shapes her current role. "As chief creative officer, I oversee all of our creative endeavors. With our film and TV stuff, I am his producing partner. We do everything together. I go out there and basically try to find projects—movie projects—that make sense for us, for me, for him, for the brand. The great thing about someone like Pharrell—whose main job is music—is when he's doing film and TV, it's awesome in the sense that there is not a lot of pressure to just get a bunch of projects going. We can be very selective. While it is an important part of the company to concentrate on, we don't have this sort of bottom line where we are like, 'We have to do X amount of movie projects a year, we have to do X amount to TV projects a year.' It's like, if it makes sense, we'll do it."

When asked about what filters guide the partnership process, she says, "I think it's really all gut, as silly as it sounds. It's not really about any kind of market research or algorithms or how successful a brand is. All those things, they freak Pharrell out, they freak me out; that is not how we make decisions. Both Pharrell and I . . . the way we approach work is, 'Does this feel good?' Then this must be the right thing that we are doing.' Because it feels good regardless [of] whether it's successful or not, [and] that's a win for us. And that is really a blessing, especially for someone like me, who is a creative."

Those gut instincts paid off when it was time for Mimi to produce her first music video for Pharrell's hit song "Happy," which became one of the biggest cultural phenomena of the last decade. Her lifelong experience as a storyteller and passion for diversity had prepared her perfectly for this moment. And by baking i am OTHER's core value of celebrating individuality into the concept from the beginning, she was able to help create something that felt authentic and accessible to millions around the world.

Mimi says, "We know what we stand for at i am OTHER; we know we stand for individuality. People expect new ideas from us, things that haven't been done before, but as you know, almost everything has been done before, or that's what it always feels like. But I think the only way to do things that are different is to innovate. And in order to do 'new ideas, or a new spin on ideas,' which is basically the way that we look at the world, there almost has to be a little bit of fear in deciding to do the project; it has to feel kind of risky. For me that always feels like a good place. I always knew that personally when something feels risky, a little crazy, I am like, 'OK, we are on the right path,' because if it doesn't feel that way, then that means it has been done before.

"I had never done a music video before. That was my first time working on a project like that, and it was sort of the same thing. I approached it as a journalist, [but] Pharrell had a different idea of what he wanted to put in that music video. . . . I just remembered in the movie [*Despicable Me 2*] when the lead character, Gru, realizes he is falling in love, he starts dancing, and when 'Happy' plays in the movie, he's dancing down the street in scenes of happiness. I was like, 'That's what you should do! You should do that scene from the movie; we should just sort of replicate that.' But again, that came from a place of good storytelling."

Mimi's intuitions on the concept of the video proved to be spot on, but it was the creative audacity of its execution that made the video so remarkable. Proclaimed as the world's first 24-hour music video, it features an array of people dancing including Pharrell, Magic Johnson, Jamie Foxx and actress Miranda Cosgrove, in various environments. Fans were able to watch clips across multiple media outlets or view the full video on the main website, which was time stamped to show when people were filmed over a 24-hour period.

"I remember getting the treatment and getting to the page where they had the twenty-four-hour concept, and I remember slamming my computer shut, like, 'Oh my God!' It was like the biggest idea in the world. It felt so crazy to me, and honestly I didn't know how this was going to get done. 'This sounds so crazy and probably impossible, but fuck it! Let's figure this out! If the directors feel confident they can figure it out, I'm just going to go ahead and believe it.' Maybe that was the naïveness, maybe that came from not knowing how all of this would work, but it felt crazy. It felt like, you know, 'I don't know how we are going to do this.' I think a lot of times that's kind of how we approach things."

She continues, "The directors [the Paris-based directing team We Are from L.A.], they were the ones that came up with the twenty-four-hour concept that this was born out of. You know, the directors were just awesome, but I remember being like, 'This [is] a family movie, so let's have everybody, let's have kids, let's have older people, let's have all shapes and sizes!' Even to the point, I remember telling the casting girl, 'I want different shades of black people, and not everybody can have a weave. I need, like, natural hair; I need braids!'

"I was so explicit about that because I was like, 'Let's make sure we are representing everybody and making it really, really diverse.' The more people you include in telling the story, then the more chance you have of it reaching as many people as possible.

"But of course, no one knew it would become what it became. It felt good to know that, 'OK, we did this right. We did this in a way that everyone felt included and wanted to participate in it and show that they were also happy too.'"

With the massive success of the "Happy" video, it made sense

that the next natural progression would be a film, and so in partnership with writer/director Rick Famuyiwa, as well as producers
Forest Whitaker and Nina Yang Bongiovi, Mimi and Pharrell coproduced the movie *Dope*, a coming-of-age film about an African
American teenage nerd who, along with his eclectic group of friends,
navigates the dangers of a tough L.A. neighborhood while pursuing
his ultimate goal of getting accepted into Harvard University. The
film creatively ties together several of the themes i am OTHER
celebrates—individuality, education, and openness—into an entertaining film that resonates with many young people who otherwise
don't see themselves represented in the stereotypical ethnic imagery
of most Hollywood films. As a result, the film has developed a cult
following among legions of youth who identify with that sense of
otherness.

From the beginning, the film was a critical success, winning rave
reviews and multiple bids at Sundance. However, it was the response
at Cannes that shocked Mimi, and a conversation with Pharrell that
reminded her about what's most important and the impact her work
should have in the world.

She says, "We did *Dope*, and we already had the success at Sundance, but we got into Cannes, and I was really shocked. And then
we're there at the premiere, and then I started to get really nervous
because I knew that when the French come, when they don't like a
movie, they boo it. So I was paranoid, and I was like, 'Oh God! Please
don't let them boo our movie!' And Pharrell was next to me, and he
looks at me and says, 'Calm down!' He was like, 'We are at Cannes,
we have a movie here. Who cares? What difference does it make? It's
going to be fine; it's going to be fine.' Look where this movie took us.
He was like, 'You're looking at this the wrong way, Mimi.'"

She continues, "You know, sometimes you just have to be reminded that it doesn't matter if it's successful or not. Like, did it feel
good making it? Was there purpose in it? Can this inspire people

in some way? For me, always when I've created any kind of content, told any kind of story, my three rules are I want to educate, I want to entertain, and I want to inspire. If the content that I have worked on [has] those three things, then I am good. Then I feel like I have done my job, because those are three things I think are successful storytelling. But regardless of how big your audience is or how small it is, you can do those three things, and then I think it's a win."

After *Dope*, Mimi expected to build the film and TV division doing indie movies, slowly graduating to studio movies. However, it was a chance meeting that gave her an unexpected opportunity to tell an amazing story that had been waiting more than fifty years to be told. She tells the story of how she and Pharrell became executive producers on the film *Hidden Figures* with Fox 2000 Pictures, coming out in 2017—their second movie and first studio movie.

Mimi explains, "Randomly, I have this meeting with Donna Gigliotti an Oscar-winning producer. She is from New York, an amazing, amazing woman—she won the Oscar for *Shakespeare in Love*, but she also did *The Reader*, she also did *Silver Linings Playbook*. So this is someone who is like, super-established and has a legendary track record. I had a meeting with her about another project, and so we just start talking and having a really good time, and we both kinda liked each other. And I just happened to ask her what kind of projects she's working on. So she's like, 'Well, you know, I've optioned this book; it hasn't come out yet. It's called *Hidden Figures*. It's about African American women that worked at NASA; they were kind of the human computers. The black women were called the colored computers, and they hand-calculated some of our space missions, notably John Glenn's first space orbit [on the Mercury-Atlas 6 "Friendship 7" spacecraft],' and I am looking at her like, 'Oh my gosh! Are you serious?' One, how do I not know about this? And two, please, please; Pharrell will die when I tell him about this! Can we be involved in the project?

"I am like, 'We will do anything from music to screening; I'll put you on the phone with Pharrell.' So immediately, the next day, I put her on the phone with Pharrell. Anyway, long story short, we get on this movie, and I couldn't be happier, because then I get to Atlanta and Taraji [P. Henson] plays the lead, named Katherine Johnson. Octavia Spencer plays one of the other women; Janelle Monáe plays the other woman. Kevin Costner plays the head of the space task force, Kirsten Dunst another key role. So it's just an incredible cast, and one of the most amazing experiences that I've had, simply because it is just a great story, and everybody on set knew the importance of the story. You could just feel it in the energy. They were like, 'OK! We are here because we want to do this movie and these are great roles, but man, this is an important story!'"

The moment made Mimi reflect on her journey and the idea that some things are predestined. She says, "Cheo Hodari Coker is a journalist-turned-screenwriter, and he is a really good friend of mine. He always knew he was going to go into screenwriting; that was his goal. He was always telling me, from the '90s, that I'd be a great producer or writer—'whatever it is you want to do.' I was kind of like, 'Yeah, OK?'

"It seems like a fantasy, but OK. And I remember buying a couple of books at the time, maybe some screenwriting books, some producing books, but I don't think I even read them. I might have just looked through them, and they just kind of sat in my bookshelf. Fast-forward like twenty years later when the *Dope* opportunity came about and I was in L.A. shooting that. And Cheo hears about it, and he was like, 'I told you! I told you, you was gonna do all that!' And I was like, 'You did! You did tell me!' I said, 'I guess I should have paid attention!' But everything happens for a reason. Everything happens when it's supposed to."

It's clear the universe is letting Mimi know this is the work she is supposed to be doing. "I just want people to recognize that diversity is beautiful, that it's not something to be scared of," Mimi says. "If anything, it's something to seek and to appreciate because you can really color your world in a way that maybe you didn't anticipate, right? It's that childlike wonder that you have in kindergarten that unfortunately I think a lot of people lose as they get older, because they feel like that's not how they should be experiencing the world.

"And it's exciting, because of all these beautiful moments that get captured in your childhood when you are appreciating differences, that's what it is. And for whatever reason, I don't know what happens when you get older and you start to lose that childlike wonder and the appreciation, and that curiosity fades. So for me, I just want to remind people, like, 'Remember that feeling?' Everything you say you were curious about, you should look at diversity in the same way. The more you can be exposed to different people and cultures, whether it's food or different cities or different music[, do it]. What a gift to be able to experience all that diversity, and it can just inform and color who you are, right?

"I don't know if that comes from me being obsessed with stories and storytelling and starting out as a journalism major at NYU, but that dedication to just wanting to learn about the world is something that more people need to just experience. Because it's fun, really fun!"

WHY WE LOVE THIS EXAMPLE: We love this example because it shows us ways to harness popular culture to express our purpose in innovative ways. By uniting her personal purpose of telling diverse stories that educate, entertain, and inspire with i am OTHER's creative platform for celebrating individuality, Mimi has been able to tell narratives in creative ways that deeply connect the i am OTHER brand and its offerings with the hearts and minds of people around the world. In the process she reminds us we are all other, and yet we are all one.

Jocelyn Cooper

Cofounder, Afropunk

"Good Is the New Cool" isn't just an idea that we saw in mainstream pop culture. Some of the most interesting examples we saw came from the very cutting edge, the vanguard, the alternative fringes of society. One such inspiring example is the Afropunk movement, which has created a safe space for "the New America"—more ethnically, sexually, and gender diverse than ever before, where people are free to design their own cultural identities from a wide-ranging palette of influences and choices.

Walking through the fields of Commodore Barry Park in Brooklyn during the annual Afropunk Festival is to see a vision of the future of America. There are people of all ages and colors here, dressed eclectically, letting their individuality shine through in hairstyles, clothing, tattoos, piercings. The vibe is super chill, inclusive, and nonjudgmental. Lesbian couples walk arm in arm, while black skater kids practice their flips. We watch from the mosh pit as Jada Pinkett-Smith launches into a fiery tune with her nu metal band Wicked Wisdom, while her spouse, Mr. Will Smith, bobs his head approvingly from behind the soundboard. Then things get even cooler when a three-piece band of young black teenagers called Unlocking the Truth comes out and absolutely slays the crowd with the tight ferocity of their heavy metal.

The crowd goes wild. Welcome to Afropunk.

The story of Afropunk began with a young entrepreneur named Matthew Morgan, who coproduced a seminal documentary titled *Afropunk* in 2004 that tracked the nascent black punk rock movement consisting of bands such as Fishbone, Bad Brains, TV on the Radio, and many others. Matthew sought to create screenings to promote the movie, which became mini musical experiences in and of themselves, and ultimately led to the staging of the first Afropunk Festival in 2005. Over the years the festival has blossomed to 60,000 people, and headlining acts have included such artists as D'Angelo, Lauryn Hill, Lenny Kravitz, Body Count, MeShell Ndegeocello, Sharon Jones, Chuck D, Kelis, Gary Clark Jr., and Grace Jones. The common thread? All artists who have blazed their own unique musical path, refusing to be pigeonholed into either mainstream hip-hop or mainstream R&B.

The 2016 lineup included TV on the Radio, Tyler the Creator, Janelle Monae, Flying Lotus, Ice Cube, the Internet, Gallant, Cee-Lo, Fishbone, George Clinton, Living Colour, and Saul Williams—some of the most influential artists performing today, side by side with the legendary artists that have influenced them. It is a testament to Afro-punk's rising star that the lineup doesn't just reflect the cutting edge of black culture, but the cutting edge of *American* culture, period. This is the new Harlem Renaissance, coalescing the worlds of music, art, and film into a scene that has now expanded to such diverse threads as the nuanced comedy of duo Key and Peele, contemporary artists like Sanford Biggers and Wangechi Mutu, and filmmakers Ava Du Vernay (*Selma*) and Ryan Coogler (*Creed*). And let's not forget the ul-timate stereotype breaker, President Barack Hussein Obama himself.

Matthew's cofounder in Afropunk is Jocelyn Cooper, who has been there since the inception. She talks about how her earliest in-fluences were her parents, especially her father. "Each day my life's work comes from being inspired by my father, who worked for a company called Shaker Brewing Company, a very famous beer com-pany in the '70s in New York. My father was the community devel-opment person and helped shape Shaker's support of theaters and galleries. He inspired me to do the work that I now do around the idea of using entertainment as a medium and as a powerful form to influence and to 'edutain' [mixing education and entertainment]. That has always been in the forefront of my mind."

Jocelyn has had a checkered career working in the music busi-ness for twenty-five years, at some pivotal moments in culture. She says, "So I worked for record companies and publishing companies, and worked for L.A. Reid. I ran the A&R department at Universal, and I always knew how powerful the 'entertainment' side was. And being able to use that for good versus evil has always been my goal. I'd been sort of involved in transitional cultural points like signing D'Angelo and ushering in neo-soul. Or at Universal, signing and working with Cash Money, helping to usher in the new hip-hop-soul movement and blow that up in a way that it hadn't blown up before. Now [Universal] continue[s] to have their legacy with Drake and Nicki Minaj, and they monopolize hip-hop. So I had seen the

WE ARE A PLATFORM FOR

Freedom of Expression

JOCELYN COOPER

power of what happens when you have obviously great music, fashion, and culture collide."

Jocelyn's time at the epicenter of popular black culture helped her realize how it could be used for good—and how it could be exploited. "When I was working for Universal, I was sitting in meetings with folks who weren't necessarily interested in the culture but more in the bottom line," she says. "You have to make decisions on culture and music around what is selling, and sometimes the lowest common denominator . . . and it's heartbreaking. You know, getting back to my family's work at things political and empowering talented people of color; it was really disheartening to be a part of destroying it on some level. I remember a video that came through: two kids, who I can't remember the name of now, and in the video there is a seven- or eight-year-old girl who had on gold shorts, and she was carrying a little boy in a red wagon, and the statement they were making was this little girl was the hoe and the boy was the pimp. I remember saying, 'I actually don't want to be a part of this!' There was no way. My parents would be ashamed."

There was something special about the early days of Afropunk that made her realize that it was different from just another ephemeral music genre or scene. She says, "Afropunk was very different because it was happening on every single level, from fashion to lifestyle to comedy—just across the board there was a cultural shift. And for me that was the most exciting piece of it. I was like, 'This is bigger than hip-hop, this is bigger than anything I've ever seen, because it is happening on a level around history, around identity.' I started to see it with black kids on skateboards in Brooklyn. The word 'punk' is a word that freaks people out, but then to see the shift where kids were identifying with that as who they are? It's an amazing journey, because it's positive."

As Afropunk evolved from a film to a festival, it became something much larger that encompasses editorial, social media, and much more. Jocelyn tells us, "I mean, we happen to be a platform for freedom of expression. The festival itself is just a celebration of that. There's this notion that people of color, black people in particular, are homogenous—there's either the hip-hop box or everyone else. I think what Afropunk has done is opened up the dialogue that there is more than just two groups and a monolithic approach to blackness; and that is obviously pervasive with the president, and with *Hamilton* . . . but I think Afropunk for young people is how they see themselves. Millions of them. And globally too, as we are taking the festival around the world. We are in Paris, we are in London, next year we'll be in South Africa and Brazil; you see the need for the platform."

This pretty much sums up what Afropunk's ethos is: the home for the alternative Black Experience, the one you don't see reflected in mainstream media. It is a beacon for those who have felt disenfranchised by pop culture and who don't feel like they fit into easy categorization based on their race or gender. Jocelyn talks about a couple moments where she realized that something bigger was happening, taking it from a niche scene to something bigger.

She says, "There was a moment at the festival when we went from, I think it was 10,000 people to 30,000 people a day. And that happened in 2012, and we had almost lost everything in 2011 to the hurricane [*Sandy*] . . . it just all just came together in a moment. And for me personally, it was D'Angelo playing Afropunk because I have been on this journey with him since he was seventeen years old, as his publisher. So to see him performing at the festival, and the set that he did at Afropunk where he didn't do any of his music, where he did covers of Fishbone and Sly Stone, the pioneers, the Afropunk originals, with The Roots? That was a magical moment for me personally."

In addition to the 60,000 people at the event, Afropunk has a reach of more than 4 million influencers online; they are the ones on the cutting edge of culture, seeking out new art forms and sources of inspiration that speak to their experience. A recent survey of their audience showed that 68 percent purchased books regularly, 38 percent had passports, and 40 percent defined their race as multiethnic. Moreover, 90 percent of them had "some college" (versus the average of 57 percent in the general population). But 45 percent said "brands didn't get them," showing that the opportunity to connect with them still exists. Brands have stepped up, though; Red Bull has been a sponsor, as have others, such as MillerCoors.

Jocelyn talks about what makes for a successful partnership with their community. "Red Bull really has a team of people that really loves the black culture, and we've been working with them now for four or five years. That's a company that invests in culture long-term. We've worked with them on many things, in particular Red Bull Sound Select, and we've put so many artists through that, everyone from Cakes Da Killa to Unlocking the Truth, Leaf, Princess Nokia . . . a list of acts who are starting to resonate, starting to make some noise, that are helping to shift culture in a really positive way [and] that are getting support from that program. . . . When Red Bull invests in something, it usually invests long-term; when you build something with the community, you have got to do it long-term. We've partnered with MillerCoors, who have been amazing. But we haven't had more major brands come on to work with us in that way, but I think we'll get there. We are still fighting and working to get there."

And Afropunk has now found a way to turn the appeal of its festival to spark even more social good. Jocelyn tells us, "Last year, we started our nonprofit organization called Afropunk Global Initiative, and 16,000 kids went through that program doing community service in order to earn a ticket into the festival. Those kids did everything from going to community board meetings to making homeless kits for homeless people—kids actually sitting down for an hour talking to a homeless person about what's going on with them. And that kind of work, which is supported by the mayor's office in New York and Art for Amnesty with Amnesty International, is really important."

Afropunk's culture of inclusiveness and tolerance has even greater resonance today, with its ability to create safe experiences for young kids under attack. "We just came back from our show in Atlanta, where 70 percent of the audience was LGBTQ kids, couples in the South where today they are being ostracized because of who they are, with North Carolina and other states legislating against the freedom of folks. To be in a room with that group of folks . . . you are like, 'OK, all the hard work we put in there comes together in a moment, in an energy.'"

And as Afropunk spreads its wings and travels to new countries, the DNA of what they stand for has found new fans in other communities around the world. "We had 6,000 people in Paris this year; we'll have 10,000 in London," Jocelyn says. "It's so needed, people are so excited. Because of the African diaspora and the Caribbean diaspora there, France is really changing and people don't know how to handle it. There's nothing like Afropunk in Europe at all; the people really rally around. . . . You got folks that are coming from Germany and Amsterdam and . . . everywhere that come to Afropunk Paris shows. It's beautiful."

WHY WE LOVE THIS EXAMPLE: In an era where race and gender are ever more politicized, Afropunk provides a safe space for all those millennial and Gen Z kids who don't quite fit in anywhere else to freely express themselves. Against the backdrop of #BlackLivesMatter and battles for bathrooms breaking out in the South, having a place like the Afropunk Festival, where transgender kids of color can walk around hand in hand with the ones they love, is hugely important. As America approaches becoming a majority-minority country by 2050, Afropunk is the shape of the future: vibrant, confident, inclusive, and supercool.

5.
DON'T ADVERTISE, SOLVE PROBLEMS

Marketers have access to so many tools in our toolbox, but all too often we rely on the same ones over and over again (banner ads, coupons, direct mail) without questioning their efficacy. What if we started using all the tools in our toolbox to come up with something different?

In this section we look at new models of creating content and experiences that are either useful or delightful and that help solve problems from "the Everyday to the Epic."

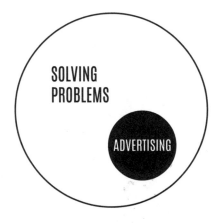

We learn from former Citibank CMO Elyssa Gray about how their investment in the Citi Bike program in New York has led to significant returns for the brand—and created a new public transport system that is now part of the city. Peter Koechley, Co-founder of the media company Upworthy, shares how they're creating a new model of positive content that brands can align themselves with. And we meet Marco Vega from the small agency We Believers, which created edible six-pack rings that can help save marine life— an idea that has taken the beer industry by storm.

Elyssa Gray,
VP Brand, Betterment

We live in a time when we are bombarded by commercial messages—some estimates say more than 5,000 a day. Our cities have turned into cluttered spaces where brands jostle for position on every available space. What if there was a wiser, more useful way to spend all those dollars? Elyssa Gray was the Head of Creative and Media at Citibank when they embarked on a journey that would change the face of New York City.

Of all the case studies we have explored, the Citi Bike story may be the one that best embodies how a marketing investment in a community (instead of in advertising) can reap amazing rewards for a brand.

The story begins with the financial crash of 2008: Citibank took an estimated $476 billion in taxpayer bailouts, more than any other bank. Its brand was in the doghouse, along with many of the other banks involved in the meltdown. Fast-forward to 2012, and Citibank gets a call from NYC mayor Mike Bloomberg's office, asking if they would be interested in underwriting the bike program. After some haggling, Citibank came on board to the tune of $41 million over a six-year period (MasterCard also came on subsequently to underwrite the payment system for around $6.5 million).

For those unfamiliar with the program, the concept is simple. Members pay an annual fee of $149, which enables them to rent bikes from stations positioned strategically around Manhattan (and some parts of Brooklyn) for an unlimited amount of rides per year—the only limitation being that each ride lasts no longer than forty-five minutes. Alternatively, for those looking for a shorter-term commitment, there are also twenty-four-hour and seven-day passes as well.

Elyssa Gray, who was Citibank's head of creative and media at the time, was one of a small group of people involved in the project from its inception. She took some time to talk to us about how it all started. She says, "It was definitely hard. It was a bit of an unknown. It was a small group of people who developed the business case for why we thought this was worth taking that leap. There definitely were a lot of concerns around safety, for instance; but we really did our due diligence with the city, with other bike-share programs, and it turns out that accidents go down with bike-share programs.

"Once we demonstrated the value of it, because it was a large investment and it was a multiyear deal, which we don't tend to do . . . people got comfortable. It wasn't easy to sell it, but people definitely saw the value."

She explains how this small team of people managed to stay passionate as they developed the program: "Our brand was at a place where, in our hometown of New York, we wanted to make sure we were doing something unique and disruptive. This program presented itself, and at first we had the same reaction, the same fears . . . but as we dug in and really thought about what this could do, we got excited and started to feed off each other. Once we were all excited about it, and developed that business case to sell it in, that was the first step."

An important part for the New York–based team was putting themselves into the mind-set of their fellow New Yorkers—and dealing with some of the setbacks along the way. Elyssa explains, "As a marketer, for me personally, and for my team, when we thought about what we were doing, the positive impact it could have on the city that we lived in, we became personally involved. We did everything: we designed the logo, the name, the bikes, how we would launch this. . . . If you remember, we had *Hurricane Sandy* in the midst of all of this, so we got delayed; many bikes were ruined in the hurricane because they were stored in the Brooklyn Navy Yard. There was plenty of opportunity for us to be stopped, but we took it on the chin because we felt it was the right thing to do. People got passionate about it; people started raising their hands to work on the project, so that was exciting. We always say, 'We are not saving lives, but we are impacting people in a very positive way.'"

Elyssa describes the impact of the program, saying, "Awareness of Citi's association is now probably 100 percent. It's the largest and most well-known bike share in the country. More than 14 million trips taken since it launched, more than 22 million miles have been traveled, 92,000 annual members, and . . . 630,000 day or week passes [have been sold]—so a lot of participation. We wanted to make sure we weren't just putting a bunch of bikes on the street with logos on them; we wanted them to be used."

But aside from the raw impressions, perhaps the most impressive return on investment has come in the shift in perception of Citibank. Elyssa explains, "After ten months, we have seen rises of 16 percent of people having a more favorable impression of Citi, 18 percent rises in the likelihood of considering a Citi product, 15 percent increases in Citi being an innovative company, and 13 percent increases of Citi 'enabling progress.' To crown it all, there was a 12 percent increase in those who thought that 'Citi is a socially responsible company.'"

Elyssa tells us what surprised her most about the reaction to the program. "When it launched, I was truly amazed and eternally satisfied that New Yorkers totally embraced this. The creativity that people have had with Citi Bike, whether it's their Tumblr pages, people getting their wedding photos on the bike . . . I think how it's part of New York City now, which is so phenomenal. I think there was even something in *Vogue* or [on *Today*] about how our blue was the 'it' color for spring! The way it just totally got into pop culture so quickly has been really fun. The response from New York has been so amazing."

Celebrities such as Leonardo DiCaprio have been spotted on the bikes, and Bruce Willis rode one onto the set of *The Late Show with David Letterman*. The program has connected culturally cool neighborhoods in Manhattan and Brooklyn in new and accessible ways, opening up the fabric of the city and allowing for new cultural exchanges. In fact, in addition to the branding on the bikes and bike stations around New York, and the millions of social media impressions, probably one of the biggest upsides is that "Citi Bike" has now entered the popular vernacular.

Many of the strongest critics of the big banks comprise exactly the kind of demographic that uses Citi Bike—young, urban, socially conscious people, for whom the financial crisis spelled disaster for careers and jobs. Citibank could have used that $41 million on advertising to try and shift public opinion; instead, the Citi Bike program seems to have shifted it far more effectively and meaningfully than anything from an advertising agency.

Elyssa reveals that the program also had a profound impact on employee pride. She says, "I'm a firm believer that our marketing efforts should make people really proud of what we do, and this does give them company pride; so many people have come to me, and they want to get involved. Driving employee engagement is critical, and this is a great opportunity for our employees to feel what we do in a very unique way. We had our one-year anniversary, we gave out annual passes, and it's a real feel-good for those who work in New York (and we just launched a bike share in Miami)—so they can see what Citi is doing for those cities."

The brand-building program has also had some positive effects on Citi's business as well. "We offer our customers a fifteen-dollar statement credit for use toward the program when they use their Citi card to buy their annual membership, and we had some great redemption. So even though brand-building and perception was the primary goal, we are seeing directional lifts from a business perspective." As of today, roughly 30 percent of the Citi Bike annual memberships have been purchased with a Citi debit or credit card.

Elyssa talks about how this program was different from what Citi had done traditionally, saying, "I look at all of the marketing tools that are available to me, within my tool belt, and each one can do different things—some [that] drive awareness or bring you information, and others [that] bring you an emotional connection, which has a great impact, in a real, authentic way. The culture now is so much more about giving back, and people expect that from the companies they do business with."

She goes on to say, "What was so unique about this program was not just that it allowed greater coverage from an advertising and marketing perspective, but it linked so directly to what the Citi brand has stood for over 200 years, which is 'enabling progress.' And that it added such amazing utility into people's lives. That's the secret sauce . . . that's when the magic happens. This is bringing a new form of transportation to the largest city in America. We're really proud of being part of this movement and bringing this program to New York.

"I think about the type of engagement we're having; we're connecting with people on such a human and emotional level. We have made people's life better, and when you can make an impact on a person's life in that way, as a brand, as a company, that's much more powerful than just seeing a billboard on the side of the road. There are times when we have to 'tell,' but we'd rather 'show'—and this is a great way to do that."

Elyssa has since left Citi to join the financial start-up Betterment as Vice President of Brand, but it's clear that she has great pride in what her team was able to accomplish with the Citi Bike program. Her parting thought? "I think all of these brands you are exploring in the book are all about putting the customer first; we're not thinking about ourselves. Yes, we have to link and label back to the brand promise, but we approached this as New Yorkers who would participate in the bike-share program: What would we want?"

WHY WE LOVE THIS EXAMPLE: Citibank could have spent its $41 million on "perishable" advertising and media. But by thinking of "Citizens, Not Consumers" and empathizing with their needs, they made a huge, tangible difference to the community they were part of. In a world where public infrastructure is crumbling, such public-private models could pave the way for new brands to engage communities in new and meaningful ways.

Peter Koechley

Cofounder, Upworthy

The oversaturation of commercial messaging doesn't get any better when you look at content on the Web. Here's a startling fact: every second one hour of content gets uploaded to YouTube. That's a decade's worth of content a day. More than any human being could ever consume in a lifetime. In today's frantic media universe, there is a lot of sound and fury but sometimes little meaning. One of the standouts in this new media world is Upworthy, which has built an enormous following around creating meaningful, nourishing video content—that just happens to get massive, viral-worthy engagement around the world.

They've been called "BuzzFeed with a soul"; they are the masters of writing stories with irresistible headlines to draw you in—but then also give you stories so inspiring that you can't help but share them. Perhaps that is part of the secret of their success; they currently have more than 14 million monthly unique users, generating more than 250 million video views per month.

We met with the affable Peter Koechley, one of the cofounders of Upworthy, to talk about their philosophy and how they got started as a media company with a mission.

Koechley says, "I think it's rare for media to be actually mission-driven. A lot of people are in media for the right reasons, but when you look at media companies, most of them are not driven with an underlying purpose. For us, purpose came even before the form of a media company. My cofounder and I were sitting around in 2011, before we launched, and we just had this feeling that the whole media ecosystem was changing. And it was going from newspapers to newsfeeds; it was my cofounder, Eli Pariser, who first had the realization that actually the stories that matter in the world are just going to disappear if the only way you see them is if your friends want to share them.

"The reason that's true is that it's not because people don't care about these stories, but it's because those stories have never had to be great stories. When you can put something on the front page of a newspaper, when you can dictate that it's at the top of the newscast, you can put your finger on the scale and kind of force it on people; and then you actually give people the choice [of] what to pay attention to. They're going to pay attention to great, compelling stories first, and important stuff kind of second. People don't seek out important things. They seek out great stories, they seek out great culture, they seek out connections to other human beings, and you have to actually embed meaningfulness and importance in those interactions and those stories in order for them to thrive on their own.

The stories didn't have to compete before, and now they would.

"And so the only way for society to actually get the nourishment it needs (because I think people have this hunger for meaning and a hunger for purpose), you need to make the stories and issues and the topics actually compelling and great and surprising and delightful and wonderful. And if you do that, people will flock to them."

Upworthy is a great example of how to "Lead with the Cool, but Bake In the Good." It is one of the modern-day masters in media about how to wrap a meaningful message in an attractive story and deliver it seamlessly to a hungry audience.

Peter says, "We say a lot that Upworthy is premised on two beliefs about human nature. One is that people are better than they get credit for [being], and the other is that they're worse than they get credit for [being] in any given moment. And so, every person, myself included, we go through a day making a thousand short-term bad decisions that maximize shininess and delight over substance and purpose and meaning, but at the end of the day, I will feel empty, and I will feel hollow, and I'll feel like I'm lacking something deeper and richer, and that feels bad.

"And if you can actually connect people with things immediately, with a sense of something that is interesting to see—it's great, it's compelling, it's fascinating, it's cool, it's hip, whatever, and then you deliver, almost by surprise, 'That was surprisingly nourishing. That actually changed how I think about things. That actually touched me on a deeper level,' you build a bond with them. That's what people really want, even if they don't seek it themselves in any given microsecond."

Peter talks about how his own habits as a media consumer guided the form of what he and his cofounder wanted to create: "It's a thing that I feel really personally, because I'm not a great media consumer. Most of my critiques about myself are about how little I read, and how I wish I was just a voracious consumer of information.

I'm actually not. I'm busy with my life, I have kids, I run a company, and I let that get in the way. I kind of wanted to create a media company for people like me. Because I can get lost and sucked down into the inanity and the pettiness of life, the sort of pedestrian day-to-day. And I really crave that feeling of deeper purpose and meaning.

"I get it when I'm with my sons and they're being amazing and tomboyish and great, but at the larger level, I want to be drawn towards the best version of myself, and I'm just as attracted to the shiny objects as everyone else. And I'm also not from a religious tradition. There's not a part of my life or my week that holds me to a commitment. So I felt like there must be a lot of people like me, and if we could create a media company for them that drew on their natural human desire for entertainment and engagement and surprise and delight, but actually channeled that towards the better version of themselves—the one that cares about other people, the one that thinks about big issues, the one that helps somebody else in the world—then it's actually a real service to every person we touch, and it's worth starting a business.

"So we hired a couple of curators who were going to help find the stories from the web, and we gave them the mandate to look for things that if a million people saw them, the world would be a better place. And people interpret it very differently from each other—and we were fine with that. We started with the mission of 'How do we get people to pay attention to really important issues? How do we make them compelling and interesting and enjoyable?' And we realized that a big part of the answer is by adding a bit of hope to the story. So I think we're believers that the combination of purpose and hope makes things dramatically more sharable and gives you the opportunity to touch a lot more people.

"I think the other thing that we get a lot from our audience is, 'Wait, I thought you guys were all positive. This is about prison reform. This is not positive.' And our take there is that we're not all positive. I think the things we try to avoid are disempowering, overcomplicated, forbidding, and sort of hopeless. We did a thing on suicide the other day. Not a positive topic. But it was about the semicolon tattoos that people are getting, and one of our writers saw the tattoos, researched, and figured out and discovered that . . . they're tattoos that people get after they've seriously considered suicide and then decided to continue their life. So they're saying, 'As the author of my life, I'm not ending the sentence; I'm going to continue.'"

Upworthy's willingness to deal with some of the darkest parts of humanity in a positive manner is a great counterpoint to those who call the content provider "smarmy" or "smug." Peter says, "It's beautiful! And it's an example of hopeful and inspiring, but looking straight at the existential darkness of suicide, which is a major problem in our society today. So I think we do as much of that. We're not Pollyannaish about the world. We just think that if somebody reads one of our stories and leaves it kind of leaning back or slumping back in their chair and wanting to get back into the bed they just got out of, we haven't done any good in the world. We want active emotions. We want to make people feel activated. The word we use for positivity is 'elevating.' Sometimes it's inspired and lifted up. Sometimes it's like an elevated heart rate. We want to get your heart going."

Part of the success of Upworthy has been its very quick and adept mastering of one of the most powerful forms of storytelling for this audience: mobile video. Peter tells us, "Videos are a huge part of what we're doing, and they're growing every day as a percentage of what we do. The stories on the site are basically all original in one form or another. The videos are licensed videos from tons of partners, and then we make our own as well. It's probably three-quarters licensed and one-quarter originals, something like that, but it's something that will shift over time. Licensing the other videos is something that we believe in. It's a part of being a mission-driven organization. As a media company, we should make all of our original videos, and we can monetize them better . . . there's all sorts of business reasons for it. [But] as a mission-driven company, if I'm an Upworthy fan and I get a video that some individual made that's great, or one of our media competitors made, or it was from some TV show, I'm happy as a fan. If it makes me care about something or feel something, it doesn't really matter. It's only in the interests of the company that makes us want to do more. . . . We're actually doing more and more original stuff because we feel that we can actually tell some stories that other people are missing, that we feel that can be added into the conversation. But every time we see a great story that somebody else had started, then we can just lift that up. We're great with that."

There is great potential for Upworthy to be the "Netflix of good news," finding and curating the best videos from around the world, as well as producing their own original content to create a portfolio of great stories for people to access. "We think a lot about Netflix," Peter says. "Our strategy to date has been, 'Let's really learn about what people like and want. Let's really build data and technology and a huge audience and study what works and what doesn't.' And now we're in the *House of Cards* era where we're making our own stuff that is much better than it would be, because it's built on four years of understanding.

"This is really a golden age of media. And I think one of the things that's making it that is we have more access to data and more access to audience feedback than we've ever had before. There was a time in storytelling where you were sitting around a campfire, and you [could] tell when people [were] nodding, when people [were] tearing up, when people [were] standing up and walking away because they [were] bored, or somebody [fell] asleep and [fell] off the log. Then there was this weird couple-hundred-year era of media where you would print something [that got] totally disseminated, and you had no idea [what happened to it]. So people stopped caring whether the audience cared. I mean, live musicians could still tell, stand-up comedians could still tell, but not if you were a newspaper writer or even largely a TV producer, though they still had some data.

"So we view this moment where we can say, 'I have a draft of a story. I can show it to my editor and my editor can give me some notes. I can also show it to a thousand random people on the Internet and see how they react to it' [as] a creative opportunity to see what works and what doesn't. And I trust my own creativity to a certain extent. But I actually trust the aggregate view of a thousand other people a lot. I think if they're all bored and they all don't read more than halfway through, then I can think it's great, but I'm probably wrong. And so we view the interplay between real-time data and audience feedback, and human creativity and ingenuity and intuition; both of them are incredibly valuable. And the real art is breaking up the process so you use data and technology in the moments when it can be the best solution, and you use human creativity when there's no substitute for that. So it's in the mixture there."

Upworthy has successfully partnered with brands ranging from Unilever (with whom they did a story around global warming) to media network the CW (to talk about early detection of pancreatic cancer).

"We're building our business at the intersection of two huge forces," Peter says. "One is this shift among brands to purposeful messages. They know what it's all about, but they know that if they want to reach millennials (and really all modern consumers) then they have to speak with authenticity and meaning and purpose, or they're just not gonna care. So that's a huge shift for them.

"Then the other is this huge shift from basically all other forms of media to mobile video. Mobile video is incredibly in ascendance, and as TV declines and other things decline, it skyrockets upwards. So brands are having a harder time reaching people on TV. They're facing ad blockers and other things that may interrupt their form of advertising and make program interruption kind of difficult. What we do is we create branded, sponsored content, stories with brands that people organically want to share themselves. It's content that is designed to be actually satisfying, because it's filled with purpose and because it's a great story."

Peter talks about some of the examples of brands Upworthy has worked with that have done it right: "We have this video series called Humanity for the Win. And Dignity Health said, 'We like this series; we want to align with it. Do you have something that's related to the medical field a little bit?' And we said yes. 'Great, we'll take this one off the slate and make it and consult with you guys.' The result was a wonderful story about the e-NABLE community who build prosthetics using 3-D printers for kids around the world.

"So that's a great one. We made a great video for Whirlpool that I really liked. You know, Whirlpool is an appliance company seeking to be a lot more than that. They were focused on, like, 'You don't wash laundry just because you want to wash laundry, you wash laundry because you care about your family; care just means so much. And care comes not through grand gestures but from a million easily ignorable, underappreciated gestures.' So we made a video about this great Haitian family living in Queens, where the pretty cantankerous grandma and the teenage son and the two mums all live in the same house. And it kind of profiles one of the mums and her holding the house together. So it's like only loosely about . . . we never mention whirlpool, but it shows her taking care of the family. It shows her holding them all together, also dealing with her cranky mum and her sweet son. It's very hard work." The content went on to win many plaudits for its heartwarming tale, part of a campaign that helped Whirlpool sales rise 6.6 percent in the months after it ran.

There is a tricky balance between a brand using its resources to spark debate about a particular issue without then getting a backlash because it is seen to be exploiting the issue without providing solutions. Peter has a nuanced view about the pros and cons of this approach. He says, "I can argue both sides of it. I think if we're going to spend $100 million a year on advertising and we can get 20 percent of that to be pro-social messages that are about a more diversity-inclusive and progressive world, I'll take it. Even if it's not connected to a great CSR initiative, if it's not connected to a great system."

In addition to brands, Upworthy also does a lot of work with nonprofits, helping them get their messages out in powerful and compelling ways. "So it's about a third of our business or something like that. And we're working with the Gates Foundation, we're working with the Open Society Foundation, we're working with a lot of the biggest and smartest foundations out there. With smaller nonprofits, marketing is expensive and it's just a hard case to make. If you're the Gates Foundation and you're going to put $10 billion into global health and poverty stuff, and you actually want to shift public opinion on it, media's a great investment. If you're a small nonprofit that's either going to spend a dollar adding a bed to your homeless shelter or running a campaign with us, we tell you to add another bed. I think there's a very useful role for actually getting the world to care about issues, so we work with people who have the means and the focus in the right place to do that. One of the great things about nonprofits is—and this is true about the smartest brands as well—is they actually care about results. So we've spent a lot of time working specifically with the Gates Foundation but using it with others to develop methodology and approach that's scientifically rigorous to look at the effect of our stories on people, the impact that our stories are having. So we can look at a campaign of stories and see how they affect the people who saw the . . . how they affect the attitudinal shift."

Upworthy is also increasingly working with some Architects of Cool who, for example, may be filmmakers more versed in telling long-form stories but who need assistance in translating that into the fast-paced, short-attention-span world of digital video. "A lot of the people coming to us are filmmakers," Peter says. Kathryn Bigelow, who directed *Zero Dark Thirty*, came to us and said, 'Hey, I care about the elephants and the ivory trade. I made this amazing PSA. Can we work together?' And we [said], 'Let's do it!' Sheryl Sandberg came to us when she was doing the follow-up campaign to *Lean In*, and now we're doing more work with Facebook because they do more social marketing. People come to us. Largely filmmakers . . . come to us and say, 'I care about this issue. I get how to tell a great story; help me connect it to the world of digital mobile social distribution for that. I can tell a ninety-minute story; help me find the three-minute story in here.' I think that's the cultural community; those are our most frequent partners. We're interested in collaborating in all sorts of ways. In the past we've worked with Shepard Fairey, with his poster in the 2008 [presidential] campaign and things like that."

As Upworthy looks to the future, we discuss the potential of new storytelling platforms such as virtual reality to help continue the great work they are doing. Peter says, "We think that a huge part of our role in the world is spreading empathy, and I think media historically has been kind of civic-minded media, which has been focused a lot on getting the facts out to people and rooting out corruption at the highest levels, both of which are very important roles. I think the third role, though, is this role of empathy. Democracy is a crazy idea—the idea that I'm going to accept some compromise in my life . . . you know, that I'll pay a tax so that somebody that I've never seen and don't understand and don't care about has a better life. Like so many of the big, amazing ideas in our world, that's really counterintuitive. And it only works if you actually care about everyone. And so the fact that we can get 10 million people around the world to watch the same video that makes a group think . . . like, *Oh, I get them. They're humans, they're just like me*, that's really powerful.

So we focus on that with mobile social video. I think VR is a great extension of that, and I'm excited to see it develop."

After our conversation, we saw a powerful example of Upworthy's mission in action. Speaking on a Reddit AMA, Peter addressed the Brussels attacks, which happened earlier that day:

"I think moments of tragedy are often the most important times to spread hope. Because they're some of the hardest times to find it. Days like today are hard. The world is full of really terrible things. Not just terrorism, but discrimination, injustice, institutional racism, grinding poverty. At Upworthy, we look for hopeful stories of people making change, because to make the world work, we actually all need to do that. And if you're feeling totally defeated, you're not going to stand up and start doing something to fix a problem in your life or your town or the world.

So when something horrific like Brussels happens, we look for how people pull together in the response. Like people in Brussels using the hashtags #IkWillHelpen ('I want to help') and #PorteOuverte ('open house') to offer shelter to those with nowhere to stay. We don't want to amplify the hatred and vitriol, we want to draw attention to the folks standing up against it."

We couldn't have said it better ourselves.

WHY WE LOVE THIS EXAMPLE: Upworthy is an example of a mission-driven media company that is challenging the norms of what "news" is and should be. Their purpose is to bring a daily dose of meaning into everyone's lives, and their results speak to the powerful desire they have uncovered within their audience for stories of purpose and optimism. We feel if more news organizations shifted away from their diet of carnage and outrage, it could create a groundswell of public opinion and activism that could help do a lot more good in the world.

Marco Vega
Cofounder, We Believers

Along with great storytelling, one of the most useful tools brands can use is the power of design. Great marketing can also be about refining the product experience to make it more useful or delightful to the end user. In this example, we look at how a tiny agency made headlines around the world when it took the humble plastic six-pack rings and transformed them into something that made a profound difference to the environment.

We meet Marco Vega at the Cannes Lions International Festival of Creativity, the biggest advertising festival in the world, in the beautiful city of Cannes, France. For this week, the city is awash in brands taking over the beach huts and yachts to hawk their wares and preach the gospel of advertising, while promotional teams hand out mini samples of everything from bottled water to bottled oxygen (we're not kidding).

It is perhaps an ironic place to talk about how brands should stop advertising and solve problems instead, but it is also a place where this theme seems to be strongly resonant in the work that is winning. Outdoor clothing brand REI's Opt Outside campaign, which closed down their stores on the biggest shopping day of the year, Black Friday, and encouraged consumers to stop shopping and go into nature, has just won a Grand Prix, the highest award you can win. And Keith Weed, the idiosyncratic CMO of Unilever, makes a presentation about how the major multinationals' five top-growing brands all have either sustainability or social conscience at their heart. Change is in the air.

Marco is exultant having just won multiple Cannes Lion awards (two golds, one silver, and one bronze) for the work that his small agency, We Believers, has done in creating the world's first edible six-pack rings for beer companies, beating out massive brands like Google, Netflix, and Audi. He speaks with the passionate intensity of someone who has found his true calling. The agency he and his partner, Gustavo Lauria, started began with the conviction that there had to be a better way forward in marketing. On their website, they make their philosophy explicit: "The best way to solve a business problem is to focus on solving people's problems and fulfilling people's needs."

The problem We Believers set out to fix was plastic waste in the world's oceans, one of the most significant environmental problems today. Research from Greenpeace shows that 80 percent of sea turtles and 70 percent of seabirds are ingesting plastic today, not to mention the massive floating landfills of trash that infest the sea, caused by more than 12 billion tons of plastic entering the world's oceans every year. And plastic six-pack rings for beer are one of the biggest culprits, well-known for entangling and strangling fish, birds, and other wildlife.

The solution We Believers came up with for their client, Saltwater Brewing—a small beer company based in Florida—was deceptively simple. Why not use the waste material used in the production of beer—the wheat, the barley—to create biodegradable and edible six-pack rings that could be harmlessly ingested by the wildlife instead of strangling them? The conservation-conscious client, who regularly worked with marine conservation charities, immediately saw the potential in the design.

Marco believes this can be the zero waste, zero carbon footprint for the entire industry. And the PR and buzz around the announcement has been huge, with hundreds of millions of positive impressions for the project in PR and social media. And in Cannes he shared with us that in the scant six weeks since the project was announced, more than 250 brewers had already contacted them to express an interest in signing up—including some of the biggest names in the business like AB InBev, Heineken, and MillerCoors. That was truly indicative that this had moved from being an idea to the start of a bigger movement.

When asked what makes We Believers' philosophy different, Marco's answer shows the conviction of his beliefs. He says, "We Believers is a place with a start-up attitude. When you truly believe and create, good things and people follow. We Believers is a place that believes in people, a place defined by its ideas and not technology as a substitute for ideas. We believe in conversations above the presentations, in 'trust us from the beginning.'" As Marco's partner Gustavo states elegantly: "For brands to be successful today, it is no longer about being the best in the world—but rather, being the best *for* the world and taking a real stance."

WE ARE FACING
AN ERA WHERE
HUMANITY WILL SHED
THOSE BRANDS WHOSE
PRODUCTS DO NOT
SOLVE A NEED.

MARCO VEGA

And when questioned about the potential for brands to "stop advertising and start solving problems," Marco's answer is equally unequivocal: "We are facing an era where humanity will shed those brands whose products do not solve a need, fail to commit to fix a cause, and fall short to fuel movements to bring people together. I believe wholeheartedly this is the way to go for business under a 'conscious capitalism' umbrella. The advertising industry, however, is proving to be deadly slow to catch up."

Marco believes that the answer to getting agencies to catch up to what consumers and brands want is to come up with a completely new paradigm and mind-set. He says, "Stop thinking like an agency. Start thinking like a venture capitalist or angel investor for good ideas. You are going to spend the next couple of months solving for that problem. You will invest a chunk of hours [in] it, so it might as well be something you truly believe in together with your client. The days of the SOW (Statement of Work) with a list of deliverables might not be gone, but you don't want to be caught in one of them. Focus on work that matters, shed work that 'needs to get done.'"

When asked about what other brands and work he thinks act in the same vein, Marco is honest enough to admit that inspiration isn't easy to find. "This is probably the question I battled the most to answer," he says. "When it [comes] to solving problems in people's lives, there are none. At least none I can think of that are not associated with an NGO or not-for-profit. We all talk about TOMS, Patagonia, Ben & Jerry's as flagships of conscious capitalism. However, none of them were to be found as festival winners. Even worse, Blake Mycoskie, TOMS founder, received an honorary award. Yet there was no TOMS work awarded in any category. So there's still a sense of [disingenuousness] going on at the festival. That is why the work we did for Saltwater Brewing makes me so proud. It's a creative idea which resulted in an invention that 'builds the brand' and 'starts a movement.' The invention is for ocean conservancy. The brand is about ocean conservancy. An authentic approach to brand building."

Marco's final advice for those in agency land who are seeking a similar path toward meaningfulness? "Do stuff that you are truly passionate about. If there is no passion, there is no drive to tear down the walls that will come towards you to squash your project. If you don't have that passion, you will get squashed. If you do have the passion, that wall, once you clear it, will make your idea better."

WHY WE LOVE THIS EXAMPLE: With Americans drinking more than 6 billion gallons of beer a year, the potential to scale this idea and make it even more cost-effective is huge. Not to mention the potential reapplicability across other industries that have similar packaging issues that cause environmental waste. It is a phenomenal example of how brands can practice "cradle-to-cradle" design principles in an enlightened way across the full life cycle of what they produce. And how the creativity inherent in the advertising industry can pivot toward solving problems through design, not just stories.

6.
PEOPLE ARE THE NEW MEDIA

n today's world, the Holy Grail of marketing is positive word of mouth. And thanks to the digital revolution, people can become your biggest advocates—at a scale that can rival even traditional paid media.

In this section, Jamie Naughton, the chief of staff of Zappos, takes us behind the scenes to show how this quirky company empowers its employees to truly bring to life their mantra of "delivering happiness," leading to legendary customer advocacy levels seen by few brands in the world. Jaha Johnson, the manager of artists such as Common and Usher, discusses how they use their work and fan base to drive social consciousness around issues such as Black Lives Matter. And Andy Tu, EVP Marketing of Defy Media, tells us how his organization is using the power of positive pranking and comedy to reach millions.

Jamie Naughton

Chief of Staff, Zappos

Study after study shows word of mouth, or personal recommendation, to be the most effective form of convincing someone to buy a product. If your friend or relative swears by it, and sings its praises (either to your face or via social media), the chances are that you are much more likely to try it out. One of the leaders in this area is the shoe retailer Zappos, which is light years ahead of everyone else.

It may seem strange that something as unsexy as an online shoe company could be thought of as being "Cool" and doing "Good," but led by the visionary CEO Tony Hsieh, Zappos has created a culture in which every single interaction with consumers is guided by the desire to improve their lives. As Hsieh summarizes simply, "Your culture is your brand."

This has led to a truly unprecedented situation where Zappos's biggest marketing asset is its army of customers who rave about the company to their family and friends, and which directly contributed to Zappos being purchased by Amazon for just less than a billion dollars.

We spoke with Jamie Naughton, who has the rather idiosyncratic title of "Chief of Staff" at Zappos—which basically means she focuses on people, culture, and community at the company. She talks passionately about the genesis of the brand, and how a lack of resources when they first launched meant they needed to become more imaginative about their marketing.

She says, "We were born right when the bubble burst in Silicon Valley, so we didn't have the luxury of millions and millions of dollars in funding that we could spend on Super Bowl ads or whatever. . . . We had no money, and no way to advertise and market ourselves. So we realized the way to market ourselves was to create a brand that customers loved so much that they [would] do all the marketing for us. At Zappos, we're really about creating story-worthy moments, whether it's for our employees, customers, or even our vendors."

For the record, Zappos does do some "traditional" marketing—whether magazine ads for products or web-traffic generation. But what it doesn't do is spend millions of dollars creating clever advertising or buying television campaigns. "Most of the money that we spend on marketing initiatives goes right back to our customers—providing free return shipping, or a lot of our packages are delivered overnight at no extra charge, sending flowers or cookies to our customers, treating our customers like they are humans. There are a million stories on how that has impacted our brand—just being good people—and how that filters out into the world," Jamie explains.

The key word to describe Zappos's interactions is that often overused term "authentic." But how does Zappos build it into the DNA of the company? According to Jamie, "We have something called PEC—Personal Emotional Connection—and it's a part of everything we do. As a manager, how am I emotionally connecting to my employees, how do I know who they are outside of the job? And the same goes for your customers—how do you emotionally connect to customers outside of the products they buy? Where the PEC comes into place with customers is that we don't have scripts and we don't have quotas. When you talk to our employees, their job isn't to sell you anything; it's to answer your questions and provide great service, and emotionally connect with whomever they're talking to on the phone."

The lengths to which Zappos goes to ensure that culture permeates every level are staggering. Jaime says, "Every single employee goes through call center training. So your first job when you enter our organization, regardless of whether you are a vice president or on our maintenance team, is to go through four weeks of call center training, learning about our history, values, philosophy, how to work our phones. And then they spend eighty hours on the phone with the customers. So 100 percent of our team is trained on how to be a call center employee. And when it gets busy for us, during the holiday season, every employee is expected to spend an additional ten hours on the phone—that's how we stay connected to our customers, and stay connected to this service proposition that we have."

The philosophy is deceptively simple but extremely radical in the context of corporate America: "If you want your employees to treat your customers well, it really starts with how you treat your employees. If you have a boss who yells and says 'Do this or I'll fire you,' you can't expect your employees to smile at your customer. Zappos is nothing more than a service company; the core of what we deliver is service. Which means it has to be about more than one department—the entire organization has to believe customer service is their job. So how HR delivers customer service to our employees is just as important as how our merchandisers deliver it to our vendors, which is just as important as how our call center employees deliver it to our customers."

The stories about Zappos's customer service are legendary—from the rep who sent flowers to a customer whose mother had just passed away to the team who bought pizzas for an entire neighborhood affected by Hurricane Sandy. There are hundreds of stories of breast cancer survivors and victims of house fires and the like—all situations where Zappos employees went above and beyond and ended up delivering something that had nothing to do with shoes: simple, human kindness.

Jamie describes how this organic approach pays dividends in ways that can't be predicted and measured—but that are invaluable in building customer loyalty. "You can spend a ton of money planning your media strategy and trying to anticipate what is trying to be the next viral thing, and most of the time you're going to fail. But if you spend money on your people and really develop an organization that has a heart, these stories just happen on their own. We could never have anticipated a 'return on investment' on a seventy-dollar flower purchase! These are the stories that make me, personally, all that more invested."

We ask Jamie what she thinks is the lesson Zappos teaches. She says, "It's that you can always add unexpected value or surprises, something funny or unexpected. If you can, surprise your customers in a good way."

We ask Jamie what her favorite story is. She says, "There's one story which nearly brought me to tears. There's this guy who called in who was on a weight-loss journey, and spoke to one of our customer service reps. He got hit with a lot of Internet trolls who made comments on his blog, and our customer service rep would get on his blog and encourage him [and tell him] how inspirational he was. He wrote this whole story about how a Zappos call center employee made him believe in himself. How can you not love that? How can you not come in to work every day and say, 'We sell shoes, and it's not life-changing and it's not changing the world, but the *way* we sell shoes is impactful, and it's changing people's lives . . . [of] the people who work here and every customer who comes into contact with us."

If you're a marketer who's been reading this book, thinking, *Hey, I work in a sector that there is nothing good or cool about. How does this apply to me?* well, the answer is right there. Ten years ago, you could have said the same thing about selling shoes—it was never meant to be world-changing or inspiring, but the way you do it can have a profound impact on people and how they see each other.

In an increasingly fragmented world, where brands are choosing to place automated voice-recognition systems or outsourced call center employees between themselves and their customers, Zappos goes in the opposite direction. It welcomes and nurtures contact between customers and the brand, instead of trying to insulate itself. Corporations allow you to forget you are a human being and hide behind these layers of process and structure; but this also makes you forget your fundamental "human-ness." And that is perhaps why so many marketers are jaded and cynical after working for corporations, being part of a system that just makes people try to "buy more stuff." Jamie laughs when we ask her what she thinks makes Zappos "cool." She answers, "What I think makes us 'cool' (even though we are the geekiest bunch of people in the world!) is we are allowed to be who we are, and that shows up in every interaction with a customer. What makes us so personable to our customers is that we are real human beings. One of our values is to be fun and weird, and all of us in this building, we bring with us every piece of who we are. We are the same in this office as we are outside this office, and that authenticity shows up in everything we do."

Think about this for a second. Millennials today understand how they are being marketed to; they understand how they are the target every single second of so many commercial messages. They can see through the "cool" stuff; they understand when a celebrity or a catchy piece of music is being used to sell them something. What Zappos does, which is to be normal and human and quirky and weird, is hugely differentiated. There's no advertising agency telling them to do this; it's just the people actually inside the company and who they really are—that's what makes people react so well to Zappos.

Zappos goes deeper than any of the other examples in this book because they forget about the "marketing" and let the people of their company do good. Having happy employees who transmit their happiness to their customers works in every industry and every environment; everyone can think of ways to add unexpected delight and surprise in their industry. That is maybe the biggest lesson that Zappos can teach us.

WHY WE LOVE THIS EXAMPLE: Zappos shows a path forward where it's not about what you sell but how you do it. In a way, that respects the basic humanity of both the employee and the customer. By being humble and positive and passionate and . . . "human." Today you cannot build a brand on advertising alone; you have to build it on something deeper and more fundamental. And there is nothing more fundamental than being "good" to someone else. And that is profoundly inspiring and exciting and different in corporate America.

Jaha Johnson

Manager, Common and Usher

Jaha Johnson believes in this age when fans are demanding more transparency and access, authenticity is more essential than ever from the artists themselves and the art they create. Jaha shares how that expectation is inspiring artists such as Usher and Common to be more open about the social issues they care about and to create music that reflects their passions and moves people to action . . . and how a near-death experience has helped him embrace his own purpose for helping others.

Jaha Johnson has worn many hats in his career: manager and creative collaborator for some of the biggest artists in the world, including Mary J. Blige, Common, and Usher; music label executive; mentor; confidante; and cultural tastemaker. But a year ago, after a freak surfing accident left him helplessly paralyzed from the neck down, lying alone on the shore of the beach, sinking deeper and deeper into the wet sand, watching as each wave of water that washed over his face seemingly brought him closer to death, none of those titles mattered. He was simply a father praying to see his son again, and a man hoping to continue a life that suddenly felt incomplete.

Jaha miraculously survived that day, and has since recovered to full health with a renewed sense of purpose and urgency that he applies to his life and work. As we sit down to talk with Jaha in his Brooklyn home, he is wrapping up a call on a potential deal for his client, hip-hop artist, actor, and activist Common. He speaks with a noticeable combination of confidence and curiosity. He has a boldness and brashness that have helped make him a respected voice in his field, but he's equally inquisitive—intrigued and inspired by the possibilities that have yet to be explored.

Jaha tells the story of the day he realized his "why," how that realization has inspired him to help use the unique power of music to engage fans in social change, what a near-death experience taught him about himself, and how much more he still has to give. As a student at Clark University, Jaha started his career interning at different record labels, and he had a pivotal turning point one day as an intern at LaFace when he was an interning for Shanti Das (the promotions person there).

Jaha says, "At the same time I was at LaFace, I also interned for a regional rep from RCA Records, and my job then was to call radio stations and get them to play the records, and I remember just hearing a bunch of records that I didn't like, and everything at LaFace for the most part I liked. So I remember I didn't really know L.A. Reid [who was cofounder of LaFace], but I was just bold and inquisitive and I stopped him in the hallway and I said, 'What do you do if you don't like what you're being told to sell?' And he said, 'The two most important roles at a record label are the man who makes the music, which is the A&R, and the man who sells the music, which is the promotion man; everything else in between is administrative. Those are people that are just to get the job done, but someone's got to make the art and someone's got to sell the art.' So he said, 'If you don't like what you're being told to sell, you need to go on the side of making it.'

"And that one conversation changed everything for me. I was like, 'OK, so what does that mean?' So then I started researching and getting into producing. I started managing producers, and that's when I got down with Noontime [Records] and I started getting into the art of making the records. And it was like a drug for me. I've never felt such a rush because I'm involved in making this. And this is going to be on the radio, someone's going to like this; this record is going to change someone's life. Because for me, you know, music has always been about the impact it has on each individual.

"I remember the first time I heard that Donny Hathaway 'A Song for You' on a rooftop in Brooklyn with my friend, and her mom had a Donny Hathaway collection, and she played 'A Song for You' and I was psyched. I couldn't even . . . I was stuck; [I'd] never heard a song like that in my life. So for me, that's a feeling I've always wanted to be a part of; I always wanted to make things that stuck with someone's soul, to their ribs, that made them feel something that made them motivated to do something different. So that was that day; that was that moment when I found my purpose: be a part of making the art and finding out where your skill set fits in there."

One of the core values Jaha embraced early on was the importance of authenticity. It has been an essential quality that he looks for in his clients and the art they create. He believes in this age when

MUSIC HAS A WAY OF SHINING A LIGHT ON WHAT'S GOING ON NOW IN A WAY THAT NO SPEECH, NO BOOK, NO HISTORIAN CAN DO.

JAHA JOHNSON

fans are the new media, they are demanding more transparency and access; authenticity is more essential than ever.

"We're in this space now that everything is about authenticity," he says. "Everybody wants to be the truest version of themselves, now more than ever before, and I think that's because on reality TV, things are more fake than they've ever been before. Everybody wants to be more real; it's like you want to be the most honest version of yourself in the most dishonest world. We couldn't be living in a more dishonest time in terms of integrity or who we are as individuals. People are really trying to clamber on to things that they really connect with.

"You know, we laugh and joke about people like DJ Khaled [the respected hip-hop DJ who has become a Snapchat sensation from his inspiring messages], but I'm so happy for him. I mean, first of all he is a great person just as a human being, but I'm happy for him because he is inspiring and motivating people. He is doing it and he is not afraid to talk about it and to let people see it. So in this time when reality TV is taking over with so many things that aren't real, when you see people living their true authentic self, that's the reality TV we are supposed to be living in. That's what we are supposed to be watching every day. Whether you like it or not, watching this guy who works so hard and is so passionate about everything he does and is working right now, those are the things you're supposed to follow, because that's real. [There is] nothing fake about what Khalid is doing.

"People want to know what's real about these artists. You want to know what they really mean, what they really stand for: 'What do you care about outside of what you sing in your songs? Is that all you are or are you more?' So I think because there are no more secrets and because there are no more walls, the fans want to know everything about you—what inspires and influences and motivate you. If they don't feel like they know you, they are not into you. And because there are no longer these walls that exist anymore, your audience knows when you're lying.

"I think that made me very conscious of the choices that I make, who I choose to work with, what type of artists . . . I want to sign, that I want to be affiliated with, because, I want to be associated with the real, not keeping it real, but with the 'real,' like that's who you are. I want to make the best version of who you are, not the best version of who you think you are."

When we speak about the seemingly recent shift of artists being more socially active, Jaha believes it's not anything new, but he does see a shift in fans' interest in the issues artists care about. He says, "There are a lot of artists who been doing that kind of work for a long time when there was no social media and there wasn't cool technology the way it is now. Now it's applauded, you get put on a pedestal for doing it. Where before, it was like people didn't care enough or it wasn't cool enough to do those things."

He believes it's a natural evolution for artists to become more socially conscious as they become older and more successful. He tells us, "I think it's a natural trend for all artists, and I credit it to age and access. As you get older as an artist, you have the benefit of being able to travel and see the world from a different view. If you have any type of soul and consciousness, you can't help but be affected by the impact of the things you see, because your box has now grown. So if you're Common from Chicago, while you may have always had some version of consciousness, it's so much different now. You don't just see when it happens in your neighborhood; you now have the benefit of traveling the world, and then it actually makes what's happening at home more important.

"When you first started as a young kid, that's not what you're thinking about. You wanted to be a star. And as you achieve success, you then have the luxury to sit back and pay attention to the things you didn't pay attention to before. Also, when you become a parent, you start to think about the world [your] kids are going to grow up in. You know, as Common sends his daughter off to Howard University last year, as Usher has, you know, a seven-year-old child and an eight-year-old child, it's like you can't help but be aware and pay attention to the world that you are bringing someone into and wonder how you can make it better."

Jaha believes music artists, in particular, have a unique influence in the lives of people, particularly youth. He says, "No one wants to hear their parents telling them what they shouldn't do. But they would rather hear it from somebody they look up to, their favorite sports star or their favorite singer. That's not a small responsibility, you know. When a pastor gets up in church on Sunday, those people are hanging on his words. His interpretation of a book tells people how to get through the week before they come back the next Sunday. That's what artists do! When they speak, the fans are hanging on their words for guidance, for information that says this is how we do it, this is what we should wear, or this where we should go. I can't imagine what that must feel like. It has to be scary to be the person that stands onstage with a thousand eyeballs on you."

Jaha believes as a manager he plays an important role in helping and challenging his artists to execute their artistic visions and make the impact with fans they desire to. He spoke specifically about his relationship with Common and their partnership together, saying, "The most valuable part of our relationship is our conversation. You know, it's like we talked about a song the other day. I told him what was a favorite song for me on his new album, and he called to tell me today, 'I played that song for Michelle and Barack [Obama] on Saturday, and they loved it.'

"He wasn't thinking about that song like that before, and he made it! Because sometimes you need somebody with an objective eye and ear to tell you, you know, 'You did something great! Nah, nah, you're taking it for granted. No, that's a great song! That's not just a song, it's a *great* song. You should be proud of that song! Don't dismiss it.'"

Jaha speaks about their recent work together on Common's latest album, *Nobody's Smiling*, inspired by Common's concern about the violence in his hometown, Chicago. That album led to the powerful Oscar-winning song "Glory," which continues to have an impact on the artist and in the ongoing fight for social justice and the end of senseless violence.

"Common is someone who always kind of spoke about these issues," Jaha says. "So he makes this album and, you know, hardcore Common fans and hip-hop fans love the album. But what's great about it was it was the beginning of a cycle that led us to the song 'Glory,' because in the theme of where he was in his life, it's like 'Glory' was the period to the sentence. Because then he goes to do this movie *Selma* about Selma and Martin Luther King Jr. After seeing the movie, he was so moved he called me and said, 'I'm going to make the end title song for this movie.' He wasn't asked to, it wasn't in his deal, and he literally put it together; he called John Legend himself.

"The reason why I said it connects to when we started with the album is, for him, when he saw the movie it reminded him how far we've come and about how far we haven't come. Some of the same things that he is talking about and referencing on his album, he was reminded of when watching *Selma*, so for him, it was like he still has so much work to do.

"And you know, that song—forget winning him an Oscar—it's more about the light that the song was able to shine on him and about what's going on. It's worth more than the Oscar, because once again, it opened up so many conversations, so many dialogues; it help[ed] shine a light [on] the movie, which was important, for young people to see that movie."

That experience reinforces the power music has to reach people in powerful ways. "I always say: 'Music is the soundtrack to everyone's life.' It's a part of every important moment. It's your victory, or it's your funeral song. It's your 'I'm in love' song; it's your 'stand up and do something' song.

"Music has a way of shining a light on what's going on now and what went on then in a way that no speech, no book, no historian can do. Kids have a short attention span, and when you can get to them in three minutes in a song what they get in a class for an hour or for a year course, you can't equate. It's like you can tell me every day to come to school and study this, but this one song inspired me the way that one class is supposed to. That's not to discount or take away from education, or discount or take away from public speakers or reading or anything like that, but songs—music—is the most motivational tool."

We also speak about Usher's active support for the Black Lives Matter movement, and how seeing another young Black male killed by a police officer inspired Usher to create a song that led to one of the biggest music events and fund-raisers of 2015. Jaha says, "With Usher specifically, it's a newer space for him to play in publicly. You know, he's had a foundation for years that people weren't aware of, doing a lot of work with Harry Belafonte, the Clintons, and education has always been a big platform for him, but once again these things weren't celebrated the way they are now.

"Last summer, we were in London making the album and another case, something just happened on the news. I can't remember which case it was; it might have been the one in North Carolina where the cop shot the guy in the back. But something happened, and we go to the studio that night and there was this track that the bands were working on, and he starts talking with Bibi, one of the songwriters on his album, about what he wanted to sing. Bibi is from Berlin and she's young. She's like twenty years old, so a lot of this she doesn't really understand, which in itself was an interesting dynamic to have these two artists writing together, one from a very informed standpoint and the other one from an uninformed standpoint.

"He made the song called 'Change' because he was very passionate about 'This has to stop! You [the police] are here to protect and serve us; you can't keep killing us!' Not all cops are bad, but this is out of hand. It's clearly a pattern with this, and it isn't the first time. And you know I always love when a song is made from a place of passion; it's what's most important to me in my entire career.

"You know, he's so charged up and excited about the song, sending it to a couple of people, and he played it for Jay Z, and Jay called him and said it was the most excited he'd been about a song that he heard in a long time. That song and that conversation ultimately led to the Tidal X concert they had in Barclays. It is because of that song. It was because Jay Z felt his passion, Jay felt moved and decided to come together to raise this money, you know, with Harry Belafonte, Black Lives Matter, to really go to support these different initiatives around the country to help change laws, to help families; and how one song can mobilize so many people and such a movement. And for him, that's probably his least successful song; the song wasn't a hit in the sense of radio play and success by the normal standards, but it was a hit and success in terms of what it did.

"You know it led the charge to them raising $1.5 million and it just brought light and awareness, and that song led to him being asked to speak on the American Justice Summit's panel at John Jay College of Criminal Justice and all these different kinds of conversations that opened up. So that one song opened up a light and a pathway to a lot of other conversations that made me proud of him, because that's what you want.

"That's the reason why I do this is to help someone execute their art to bring it to the light to effect change in whichever way. And some change will just be for fun and some change will be to move people."

A year ago, Jaha almost didn't live to see the impact he was helping create in the world. He tells the story of an accident that changed his life. He says, "So the timing of the accident was interesting. A couple of years ago I started . . . well, in 2007 I really started running, by 2009 I got into cycling, and in 2013 I decided that I wanted to do triathlons. I wasn't a great swimmer, but in that same mind-set of just wanting to do more and pushing, work[ing] through the personal challenges, it was something that I got into.

"I had started surfing a couple of years ago, because when I got into swimming, I just loved being in the water and I wanted a new challenge, so I got into surfing. So I have a surf instructor, and I would surf with him whenever I could. It wasn't every week, but I just got a new board, a small board, a faster board. So I trained that Sunday morning and then I went out to go for a surfing lesson with my trainer and just kind of went out to get used to the new board. And it wasn't some, like, amazing story where I was on this ten-foot wave. No, I didn't even get up this particular time.

"We've been in the water for a little while, getting used to the board, and a wave was coming and I didn't get up in time, so I was just kind of waiting for the wave to get past me and wait it out. And this particular time, I wasn't even on the board, but the angle of the wave hit me [and] spun me over, and I hit my head on the bottom.

"I wasn't sure what I hit my head on, but I immediately heard this 'pop,' and it was my spine, and I was like, 'Oh, shit!' 'cause I was fully conscious, and it turns me, and then I'm on my back and I'm just like, 'Okay,' but I couldn't get my head out of the water and I couldn't move. Like, I was paralyzed from the neck down. And that's when the reality set in and then everything just kind of went slow motion. I was like, 'Oh, shit! This is really happening. Like I can, like, you know, my eyes are wide open.'

"The irony of the eyes-wide-open part is when I was younger and I used to swim, I never loved swimming because the water would always bother my eyes, and every pair of goggles I got would leak, and so I didn't trust the gear. So I was an okay swimmer, but I never swam because I just didn't trust it. And you know, swimming with your eyes closed is pointless underwater, but when I finally got back to swimming a couple of years ago, I trusted my gear; I just went for it and never looked back. And when you surf, you don't have goggles on. You know, I went for it. I'm still not worried about it; water can get in anybody's eyes. But this time, I'm underneath the water and my eyes are wide open, and I could see everything clear as day. So one of my biggest fears before, being water in my eyes—specifically saltwater—it's not even a factor, and I could look up and see my body and I could look up and at first I thought it was the sun, and I believe that it was the sun at first.

"But the light just kept getting brighter and brighter as I started to sink underneath the water, because I couldn't move. And I was trying to stay calm, and I was calm. I wasn't screaming, crying—I wasn't doing anything, but I knew nobody could hear me. So I'm just under the water and I'm just looking at my body drop underneath and then in that last moment, you know, my whole life flashed before me, with reflections on everything—my last conversation with my son Jaden, everything—and then at that last moment my instructor got there and pulled me out."

That profound event has given him a stronger sense of urgency to share more of his gifts with the world. "The accident, for me, it was less about reaffirming my purpose and more about me owning up to my own purpose," he says. "So much of what I do is for everyone else. I had my own version of that in me that I've been pushing to the back, that I haven't been executing on, and a big part of that was fear-based.

"[I asked myself,] 'Why are you not following through on some of the most important pieces of the things that you really want to do, like get your book done? Finish your script. Focus on your life. You're not here to just quietly do your work and sail off into the sunset. You're here to let people know that it's okay to work hard. And that it's okay to dream big and execute and to never stop or that there's no wrong way or there's no one way of doing things, and all these things that I've learned along the way, things that I've tried and failed at or that I can help people not make some of the same mistakes, or it's okay to make some of the same mistakes.'

"When you almost die, you realize how much more living you have to do. It's like death is final on this earth, so if I was to die that day when I said my good-byes and I thought it was over, then whatever I did up to that point, that would've been how my story would have been told. And I'm pretty sure that a lot of people would've been happy with that story, but I wouldn't have been happy with that story. 'Cause I realized that day that there is still so much that I haven't done. There's still so much that I want to teach and that I want to show people; it's not for bragging or stunting, but when you see someone else do it, you have no choice but to feel like you can do it too."

That impact is already being felt on others, starting at home. "I told my son today I went swimming this morning . . . [and] he said, 'That's it?' I said, 'What do you mean by that?' He said, "Well, Dad, you did four workouts yesterday, so today you got to do six workouts.' That's what he said to me. And just for him to think like that, that's all I want. . . . That made me so proud to hear that coming from him to let me know that he is paying attention to what I do and what I say. It didn't go unnoticed. To him it was like, 'Wow, my dad did four workouts yesterday.' So that's what the accident taught me—that I've got a duty to share, to inform, to motivate the same way people did for me. It's like we have to constantly be paying it forward."

WHY WE LOVE THIS EXAMPLE: We love this example because the lesson L.A. Reid taught Jaha—if you don't like what you are selling, create something different—can be a lesson for us all. Too often, as marketers, we find ourselves trying to get others to buy into offerings that we haven't bought into ourselves. We see the offering, and deep down we question its quality or usefulness or authenticity. But yet we try to sell it anyway, and then seem surprised when people don't buy our messages or our products. Jaha's story reminds us, even if we are not creators, we have the opportunity and responsibility to work with those who are—artists, designers, developers—to create things that we can believe in, that move us, that add value to people's lives. That is where the best work happens. It is where the real connections with consumers are made, where their advocacy is born. And even when we feel like we are drowning in a world of inauthenticity, if we open our eyes, we can see clearly there is a better way.

Andy Tu

EVP Marketing, Defy Media

People are indeed the new media—the creative story-tellers, the influential amplifiers, and the everyday fans—and when they are creatively engaged around content that moves them, there is no limit to the impact that can be made. Andy shares how Defy Media engages millions of people to act for good, and how nonprofits can also use the power of content creators like Smosh and Break to expand the reach and impact of their work.

When Andy Tu says the Internet is getting a lot nicer, it may sound hard to believe. But if there is anyone who would know about emerging trends driven by young people and their activities online, it would be him. As the EVP Marketing for Defy Media, the nation's largest independent digital content provider, Andy is responsible for entertaining the coveted and seemingly impossible to capture Gen Z and millennial audiences through a suite of digital channels that will soon grow to broadcast more than one hundred shows a week in the next year, also reaching more than 100 million social media followers.

We wanted to talk with Andy about this shift to a nicer Internet and how Defy is leveraging its massive reach to engage millions of young people in more meaningful ways. As we enter the lobby to meet Andy, the lively and irrepressible Mari greets us. Officially the office manager, Mari runs the place, and does so with a dynamic sense of humor and a larger-than-life personality that, at one point, made her the star of her own digital show years ago called *Upfront with Mari.*

As we walk through the lobby, we see images from their vast collection of hit brands, such as Smosh, the Break, and Gurl and the Gloss adorning the walls. Andy shares how Defy inspired millions of people to spark a national movement of pranking people for good and why it's more important than ever for media companies to define what they stand for, and he discusses the new wave of YouTube stars who are embodying authenticity, inclusiveness, and kindness in ways that are changing the content landscape.

He says, "I've been running marketing at Defy for about ten years. Defy was this merger of two companies—Alloy and Defy. We are very *Brady Bunch.* Alloy was historically very youth-oriented and female, and you know, we were very youth-oriented and male. And we brought the company together with this idea that we could pretty immediately become the biggest independent creator of digital video.

In the beginning, online video was not only getting more popular but you could see it wasn't just a string of one-off videos; there were brands that were starting to percolate up to the top."

One of those emerging brands was being built by Anthony Padilla and Ian Hecox—two high school friends from a middle-class suburb of Sacramento called Carmichael, California—better known as Smosh. Padilla and Hecox like many teens were experiencing the daily anxiety, angst, and awkwardness adolescence brings. Also, like most teens, they had a lot of free time, and they used it to create hilarious YouTube videos featuring themselves doing random things such as lip-syncing video game theme songs. The videos they created just to make themselves and their friends laugh over the last ten years have grown to make millions of strangers laugh around the world. Smosh has become one of the most popular and powerful brands on YouTube; their videos have been viewed more than 7 billion times and, according to Forbes, made more than $10 million in 2015.

Andy says, "So a brand like Smosh, it was far beyond two guys in Sacramento; it was this content brand and it was somewhere when kids aged out of a brand like Nickelodeon. There was no place for them to go, so they went online and it was finally a home for them."

Smosh is representative of a seismic shift in the media landscape, fueled by millions of teens and twenty-somethings who have redirected their time and attention away from the traditional screens of television to the mobile screens of the digital world. A research report by Defy Media found that 67 percent of millennials said digital delivers content they can relate to versus 41 percent for TV, and 66 percent said they turn to digital content to relax versus 47 percent for TV.[1]

Andy believes viewers are living in what he calls "a 'content

---

1 "Acumen Report: Constant Content." Defy Media, October 2014. cdn.defyme-dia.com/wp-content/uploads/2015/10/Acumen-Report-Constant-Content.pdf.

democracy,' where you wake up and any given day you have pretty much full control of what you're going to watch."

And with that power to choose, one of the things that Defy noticed early on was that young viewers were increasingly being drawn to content that they found to be nicer and more uplifting. That insight led to one of the more remarkable campaigns in the digital content space: Prank It FWD. Andy says, "The kernel of Prank It FWD was the Internet was getting to be a nicer place, and there was also this backlash towards mean-spirited things. What we used to see when it was a very web-based world, meaning you went to websites like WorldStarHipHop, [was] it was like the underbelly of the Internet. The shift we started to make is that people started to consume a lot of content in their newsfeeds, and nobody wants to be the guy to say, 'Look at this guy who got his teeth knocked in' or, 'Look at this guy who [breaks] his arm.' Instead, it was like, 'Look at this positive thing, look at this amazing moment.' The formula is babies and pets dominate newsfeeds, and so as we started to see that shift, it was a very social environment. This is the stuff that we wanted to talk about, and we saw the window open for a different type of program that could start to succeed in digital.

"The flip side of the Internet getting to be a little bit of a nicer place is that pranks were getting worse. Every single prankster was doing something, and all these negative headlines were like guys walking around doing fake stabbing, but then it actually incorporated the real police. And this was getting so out of hand; people were trying to outdo each other, and so we wanted to debunk this idea that we couldn't do something nice through a prank.

"Prank It FWD basically means you think something bad is going to happen, but . . . something good happens. I mean, format-wise, we couldn't take Extreme Makeover—twenty-two minutes, super-produced, very hosted—we had to do it in a way that was still very Internet-y."

Defy launched the first round of Prank It FWD as part of its YouTube series Break, described to viewers as "unexpected goodness through positive pranks." The first prank was called "The Best Shift Ever." Andy says, "'The Best Shift Ever' was a very deserving mark that we had found through some level of casting and putting feelers out to find great people doing great things; they were hardworking people deserving of something good. We found this woman, Chelsea Roff; she was a waitress in a restaurant in L.A. and she had gone through her own struggles with an eating disorder. She'd now started a nonprofit that used yoga, which helped her on her journey to get out of her eating disorder, and she was putting dollars toward helping more people use yoga as their remedy to help people with eating disorders. So we found her and set up this idea that she was going to come into work and have this shift. There are hidden cameras all over, everybody in the restaurant was a mark, and they were in on it.

"The idea was the tips would continue to escalate throughout the shift, leading to an ultimate surprise. Chelsea starts her shift as she would any other day. As she closes out her first table, she leaves the bill for the customer, walks away, and returns to the table to find the customer has left a twenty-dollar bill for the check and $1,000 cash as a tip. Chelsea, stunned, walks back to tell her boss and other waiters."

As she moves to her second table, a married couple shares that they don't have enough money for the tip, but they have something else of value to share. They have a travel agency, and they get vouchers on all-expense-paid trips. They offer Chelsea one to Hawaii. Once again, amazed and bewildered by the generosity, Chelsea excitedly shares the news with her coworkers, who are in on the prank, and continues her shift.

Her next customer just happens to be reading a book on yoga, which sparks a touching conversation during which Chelsea shares how yoga helped her deal with an extreme eating disorder as a child, and how she uses it to help others. The customer, really Dr. Susan

Krevoy, clinical psychologist, says she has been running an eating disorder program and wants to add yoga as an offering and asks Chelsea if she wants to be part of it. Her dream job!

Chelsea's last customer pays her bill and leaves a car key. When Chelsea tries to hand the key back, the customer gently says, "No, that is your car key," and invites her to walk with her outside. Obviously confused, Chelsea walks out to find a car being driven around the corner with a red ribbon and bow around it. And of course, if that isn't enough, Chelsea is shocked to see Diana Roehl, the woman who first introduced Chelsea to yoga, get out of the car. As her friends finally tell Chelsea that these were all gifts for her, she and everyone embrace and burst into tears; the genuine joy of every single person there is evident.

It's a moving moment, and Andy gets excited telling the story of how the reaction of the viewers really showed the power of the idea, and the goodness in people. He effuses, "Oh my God! It took off! We were behind it, and we promoted it like crazy; it got picked up in news feeds and major media press. We opened the door for submissions. If you knew somebody deserving of Prank It FWD, let us know. And the response was crazy! Emails started to flood in; we got thousands and thousands of people. It was everywhere; every story sadder than the next. We started to say, 'We have to add an element [whereby viewers] can donate as we get more people watching this stuff, to try to help people in other ways that we can't just through the videos.' But also we said, 'Can we lower the bar and get people to pull their own pranks?'"

Andy and his team decided to partner with the nonprofit Do-Something.org and make a donation to them for every video view. They also invited viewers to create their own pranks. Andy enthusiastically tells the story of one group of people who wanted to create their own version of Prank It FWD: "We got this email from a woman who worked at a trucking company in Canada—like not rural Canada but not in, like, a major city—and she said, 'I saw you guys on the Prank It FWD video. I was so moved, the whole company, we threw our own internal Prank It FWD for somebody in the community. We wanted to invite somebody in the local community that's just going through a hard time or needed our help. We found that person and were curious if you wanted to shoot the video.'

"So it was this couple; they were going through tough times. He was sick, he had Hodgkin's lymphoma, and they hadn't got[ten] married yet. The couple pushed their wedding multiple times due to his treatment, and the company was going to throw this couple a surprise wedding. They found out [the groom] was a huge motocross fan, and so through calling in favors everywhere, we got in touch with his favorite rider's manager. This guy [the motocross rider] could not have been more gracious with his time, and he [was] like, 'If you guys buy my plane ticket, I'll be there!' We get him up there, [and] he shows up at the [surprise] wedding [and] gives [the groom] head-to-toe motocross gear [and then] stays for the wedding, and we captured the whole thing! We didn't actually make a consumer-facing video; we just wanted them to have a wedding video, and that we handed back over to them."

Andy speaks about the positive impact these events have on the employees of Defy as well, saying, "You want to work in a company that is not only doing stuff but feels like it's making a difference."

There was a clear indication people liked the format, Andy says, and since the first few pranks, they have "had something like 25,000 submissions!" Andy says, "We've done five rounds of Prank It FWD, including much better pranks than [the] initial ones that [upped] our game, and [we found] cool ways for brands to hop along [on] the ride with us. Our most high-profile prank, or the one that broke the Internet, [was one] we did . . . called 'She's Got It Maid,' and it was for a woman who was a housekeeper in Cleveland, Ohio."

The woman was Cara Simmons, a petite African American

woman with short blond hair, an abundance of positive energy, and a great sense of humor. She was also a single mother of three who had never had a day off of work. She was working so hard; she had actually been hospitalized several times for exhaustion. The resulting hospital bills were mounting, and she and her family were struggling to pay rent. Her boss, Mary Jo, and her sister, Glo Simmons, had nominated her for the prank because they felt she was so deserving of it, and they wanted to show Cara how much they loved and appreciated her.

Andy vividly recalls the prank: "The premise is the woman that hired her was throwing a party that night, and just needed some extra hands to get ready. After Cara arrives for work, the woman that hired her says, 'I need somebody to taste all this food.' All the food is made by a five-star chef [Manny Slomovits] in the area, [and he] takes [Cara] on a seven-course meal.'

"[Cara] is like, 'This is the best meal I've ever had.' She's taking pictures of everything, and she's like, 'My friends are never going to believe this! This is the best meal!' It's lobster, it's caviar, and then— the next part is my favorite part— . . . two masseuses come in and they're like, 'Hey, do you mind if we warm our hands up before the party begins at the massage station?' She's like, 'Are you serious?' There are these two handsome, strapping guys who give her a back rub. It's so funny."

Afterward, Cara is causally invited upstairs to look through some clothes the owner of the house is going to donate. To her surprise, she finds designer clothes all in her size—unbeknownst to her, picked out by her sister—including coats, sunglasses, and designer shoes.

Andy says, "And finally a moving guy comes and says, 'I'm getting ready for the party, and I'm supposed to drop off all the stuff. Can you help me move these boxes and start unpacking it? So she starts unpacking the boxes and she is like, 'This is my stuff,' and he shows his contract and says, 'I'm supposed to deliver this stuff. I don't know what you mean.' She is like, 'This is my stuff; this is really weird,' and he says, 'OK, well, maybe I have something in my truck that I can [use to] figure it out.' Over at the back of the truck, her kids are in it, and they jump out! She is already losing it, and he says, 'Well, your family knows something that you don't know. This house is actually your new house!' She [goes] ballistic! . . . We worked with [a] Cleveland housing association (Neighborhood Housing Services of Greater Cleveland) that did a ninety-nine-year lease as a part of it, and we were just trying to help people find ways to get homeownership."

The house, previously in foreclosure, was donated by Ocwen Financial Corporation and was renovated by Defy. Each child had his or her own room, and none of them could contain themselves, running from one fully decorated room to another in disbelief. And the final surprise: a much-needed vacation for Cara and her sister, who were given all-expense-paid trips to Mexico.

The prank was done in partnership with Barefoot Wine, which was integrated as they toasted to the new home and good fortune.

Andy's excitement as he tells the story is contagious. It's genuine and comes from knowing he was part of something that was not only good and transformative for the family but that struck an emotional chord with millions of people who inspired others to spread more goodness in the world. One of the most important things Defy understood is that by putting the idea in the hands of everyday people, they could do things with it far beyond the capacity of the Defy team.

Andy says, "With the backlog of people who then started coming out of the woodwork, sharing all the stories . . . all we [could] advise is, 'We can't do a prank for [all] 25,000, but if you use this format and find these moments of surprise, do it. There is no barrier; you can do it.' So when people hashtag us, we've had so many golden moments, like people have raised money for their janitors in their school and said, like, 'We spilled something, but the mop bucket is over there.' So he goes there, and it's full of money."

Andy believes now is a great time for storytellers to create more positive and nicer content. He sees a positivity movement among this era of creators, and it is because they are genuinely accepting, nicer, and more inclusive.

He says, "You look at Smosh; they are super accepting of people of all ages, race, gender, and ethnicity, because that's just an era they grew up in—a much more accepting environment. So we are cognizant of that, and I don't think we have to work that hard to say the voice of this brand is accepting . . . that's just who those creators apparently are."

It's that type of authenticity that is making these content creators so trusted, particularly by younger audiences. When a *Variety*-commissioned survey from 2014 asked 1,500 respondents questions assessing how twenty well-known personalities compared in terms of relatability, engagement, and generalized influence, the five most influential figures were all YouTube creators, led by Smosh, the Fine Bros., and PewDiePie—beating out traditional stars Katy Perry, Jennifer Lawrence, and Rihanna.

What these content creators are teaching brands, including media brands like Defy, is the importance of meaning and purpose, particularly when telling your brand story. Andy says, "This idea that your brand should mean something or stand for something applies to the media players too; and so I don't think it's a marketing tactic to say, 'What do we care about, as a channel, as a brand, as a programmer?' And that might manifest as, 'We care about this idea, so we made this show.' It might just be a pure form of entertainment, but it's important to be honest about what we care about: 'We are passionate about this thing, and that's what we stand for.'

"The research that we've done—people are connected to brands that have a story, and they want to know that story and they want to be connected to that story. I truly don't think that means every single thing that you do has to have a warm, fuzzy aspect, but it does mean that it should mean something."

Knowing who you are and what you stand for also drives the

partnerships Defy enters into, particularly with nonprofits. "We get pitched a lot; we get pitched from a lot of amazing groups doing amazing things," Andy says. "We've said no to some nonprofit things when we either [didn't] find common ground or shared DNA. We are not idealistic that every time we do something positive that it's a dream fit for both parties."

But Andy shares one great example of when it does align: a partnership between Made Man, a brand focused on helping men improve their lives, and Career Gear, a nonprofit that provides professional clothing, mentoring, and life skills to help men in poverty become stronger contributors to their families and communities. The initiative, called Gentleman Up, invited members of the Made Man community to all wear suits, ties, cocktail dresses, etc. to their offices on Friday, October 9, 2015. For every photo posted to Twitter or Instagram and tagged #FormalFriday, Made Man donated one dollar to Career Gear.

Andy talks more about the partnership, saying, "Career Gear helps men come out of poverty, come out of a situation where they are unemployed, and they not only give them a suit but they get them ready to reenter the workforce. For them and us, that partnership was such a great and natural alliance."

Andy continues, "There are people who come out of the prison system and they have such a slim shot at actually getting a job and staying in the workforce, so we were like, 'That's such a noble thing,' and [Career Gear] is a brand that doesn't have a huge broadcast network, we don't see them all over the place, so we wanted to tie it in a way that is super organic and also felt like the same people who are going to watch these things about men doing more should be aware of this cause. So I think that was the case; we just felt something that was really tied into what this audience was going to care about . . . something that we felt a natural inclination that we had overlap with."

For nonprofits that are looking to join with media partners to expand the reach of their message and story, Andy offers three tips: "The question is, what's your pitch? You know, are you trying to pull heartstrings? Are you trying to say we have some promotional heft? Not everybody is looking for something from you to offer, but you got to compel them to tell your story.

"And second, who are the people that have some shared DNA with you? Some of the people who pitched us, we are like, 'Hey, we love you, but we just don't know that it's going to overlap.' Nonprofits are so scrappy because their resources are historically so few. You're not starting conversations with, 'This is how much money I have to offer you; here's the talent I have to give you.' They have to come out with a different angle, and it can't always be because we are doing such great things. It doesn't matter who you are, you want to find a way to help, but sometimes you just don't have that super-shared DNA.

"Last, I'd say as you actually get to the line where you have to integrate media, talent, partnerships, you gotta let go of some control; I think in this space more so than others." Andy stresses that nonprofits need to understand what they do best and be comfortable with not having full control over the other aspects of the partnership, such as writing scripts or creative treatments. Trusting the media partners to do what they do best is what makes these things work.

WHY WE LOVE THIS EXAMPLE: It reminds us that today's digital content creators and their fans can be tremendous forces in creating more good in the real world. Their power lies in their influence, authenticity, and the credible relationship they have with their fans and followers. They can be invaluable allies for brands and nonprofits looking to drive changes in attitudes and behaviors, or simply awareness. The key for brands and nonprofits is to relinquish the traditional notions of control, and trust them to do what they do best—tell stories that entertain and move people to action.

7.
BACK UP THE PROMISE WITH THE PROOF

Today when every brand is preaching a message of positive empowerment, it is important to back up messaging with action—otherwise it will be seen either as empty rhetoric or a brand exploiting an issue for commercial gain. We live in an era when consumers not only demand transparency and accountability but are equipped with tools to call out brands that do not "back up the promise with the proof."

In this section, Laura Probst, the head of social goodness at the Honest Company, reveals how she is "reinventing CSR" to ensure her company makes good on its promise to help children's safety and health. Bobby Campbell, Lady Gaga's manager, opens up about how he helps one of the most significant musical and social voices of our time use her talent and fame to collaborate with brands to do more good. And Andy Fyfe, head of community at the non-profit B Lab, gives us insights about the revolutionary B Corps such as Kickstarter, Etsy, and Ben & Jerry's that are creating a new corporate model for "doing well by doing good."

Laura Probst

Head of Social Goodness, the Honest Company

Too often corporate social responsibility (CSR) has become a tired exercise: photo opportunities and window dressing to show the public that a company really does care about being a "good corporate citizen." But what if you could "reinvent CSR" to be a vibrant force for good, one that brings the company's purpose to life in new and unique ways? In this chapter, we meet Laura Probst, the Honest Company's Head of Social Goodness, who is doing just that.

The Honest Company is a fascinating example of what happens when an Architect of Cool decides to start her own social business. Golden Globe–nominated actress Jessica Alba (star of such films as *Sin City*, *Little Fockers*, and *Fantastic Four*) had a childhood involving asthma- and allergy-related illnesses; when she became a mom herself and was washing her daughter Honor's clothes with a detergent that caused herself to break out in hives, she had a moment of awakening. She started investigating the chemicals used in products and realized that some toxins could be labeled in misleading ways.

That epiphany led her to cofound the Honest Company in 2011 with Christopher Gavigan, an expert in how the environment affects children whose book *Healthy Child Healthy World* addressed many of the issues Alba was focused on. They were both fueled by the purpose of creating a range of safe, nontoxic baby products that avoided many of the harmful chemicals found in many other products. They wanted to create a "dream brand" that, in their own words, had "savvy style, sustainability, and extraordinary service & convenience all wrapped in a passion for social goodness, tied with a bow of integrity and sprinkled with a little cheeky fun."

They define the purpose of their company as being "to build healthier, safer families," and so far the response has been rapturous. The company's sales in 2014 totaled $170 million, and in a recent funding round, the company was valued at $1.7 billion. Of its sales, 80 percent come from an online subscription service, with the rest coming from conventional retail such as Whole Foods, Target, and Costco . The company has spent little or nothing on traditional media like print ads, TV, or out-of-home advertising, relying instead on the publicity generated by its charismatic founder (who has more than 6 million Instagram followers), as well as the strong word of mouth generated by its loyal fans.

In 2015 the Honest Company debuted Honest Beauty, a separate range of eighty-three skin-care and makeup products, with ingredients derived from botanicals and free of many of the common chemicals found in such products. Alba and her team have also lobbied Congress on multiple occasions, demanding higher standards of labeling, not just on toiletries but also on clothing and toys for children. Unlike other celebrity ventures (Gwyneth Paltrow's Goop springs to mind), part of the Honest Company's appeal is that they don't deal in rarefied celebrity aspirations but rather empathize with the day-to-day problems of all parents. And they have also tried to ensure the products remain relatively affordable and within the reach of all parents.

The Honest Company also does a tremendous amount of "Social Goodness" (their term for CSR) partnerships, focusing mainly on early child development, as well as training young people to help achieve their dreams. They partner with a tremendous range of nonprofits, including FoodCorps, the Center for Environmental Health, and Girls Who Code. In addition, they have funded things like the Honest Company Ultra Clean Room at Mount Sinai Hospital in New York City, a state-of-the-art facility that can measure the impact of chemicals in the environment on children's health, and will reduce the turnaround time for test results from eighteen months to less than two weeks.

We spoke to Laura Probst, who is the head of social goodness, about how her journey started and some of the insights she gained along the way. "I always knew that I wanted to find a career making a difference. It was how I grew up and what motivated me. I had been working before that and really wanted to do something service-oriented; I kind of wanted to go in the Peace Corps, and that kind of scared my mom," she laughs. "Peace Corps was a two-year commitment, so I thought I'd kind of go and do my own project that I could go do for several months [as opposed to two years], and then [I'd] go off to law school."

Laura's path to purpose started when she was working with a

women's empowerment organization in South Africa, helping ensure the viability of its microenterprise program through a strategic partnership with Woolworths. She says, "I did some work in South Africa with a nonprofit back in 1999. We saw that women in the program just needed to have dinner tonight. And we went up the road to a Woolworths and asked them what they did with the damaged cans and the food that was about to expire, because we needed to give our women dinner and they are dropping out of our program, and we wondered if they would consider donating it to us. And we found that this was actually quite a problem for them because they had to dispose of the expiring food, and that cost them money and resources. And they were thrilled with the idea that we might actually take their problem and turn it into something good—and make them look good—by doing some positive PR. So they gave us the opportunity to start transporting the dented food, and we saw the rates of the program go up, and the company started to ask, 'Well, what else can we do for you?'

"So for me it was a very big aha moment of, 'Oh, OK, this is a very powerful way to make a difference because you can get these huge companies which have lots of resources—actual products that I want, financial resources, talent, volunteers. So if we can just make this work for them, they're so willing to do more. And so that's really what got me on my path of creating real win-win partnerships between brands and nonprofit organizations."

In an era when many brands are claiming to do good, Laura pointed out one important fact: "I think it needs to be clear and simple. People need to very easily get it, where the money goes, and they need to relate to it, to see movement. A lot of people love the idea of doing good but can end up feeling very defeated in that journey, depending on what kind of 'doing good' you are offering them. For example, if you offer them a chance to 'do good to help cancer,' a lot of money and effort has gone into that, but we still have a very big cancer problem. If you look at things like the ALS Ice Bucket Challenge—the fact that they followed up after one year and they actually had had tangible results to show—I think that's what made it really cool."

Laura talks about how it was important to build programs that had the transparency and the accountability to show people how their contributions made a difference. She says, "People need to feel like 'I made a difference. I helped move the needle.' When they are joining in and engaging . . . you can fulfill them by allowing them to see that something real happened. Charity: Water lets you see the wells they build. DonorsChoose: if you help a classroom, you get a thank-you note from the actual kids. [Donors] need to know that all their money didn't go into a pit."

Laura brings up an important point: in a world where people may have a sense of fatigue about all the problems demanding attention, and a sense of hopelessness about whether their individual actions can actually make any difference, it is tremendously important to show the results. We call this principle Backing Up the Promise (the cause or the big idea you are inviting in) with the Proof (showing the results of all the collective action that has taken place).

Laura also points out how this translated into the actions of brands and raised the stakes for them. "In the past brands could benefit by putting a pink ribbon on their packaging," she says. "But now consumers demand more because brands like TOMS and Warby Parker have given them simple models—buy a pair, give a pair." And people say "I like that; it's simple. If I am really doing good, show me what good I am doing."

We move on to talk about her current role at the Honest Company. "As Head of Social Goodness, I oversee all of our missions' outward and internal engagement activities, from employee volunteerism to all of our philanthropy and social giving, cash and grants and product donations. All the communications around that, creating cause-marketing programs, thought-leadership opportunities, and really leading the policy-engagement efforts that bring our social-impact mission to life. It's like the head of CSR, but we call it Social Goodness because our brand is cool and has a cheekiness to it!"

We dived deeper into what Laura means by Social Goodness in the context of the company. She tells us, "Social goodness is at the heart of what the Honest Company is about. Jessica had a non-profit vision but created a for-profit business to make it sustainable. The goal was always social impact, and the company was the means to make it possible. We're not out there in all our communications or advertising talking about our social responsibility, but that's at the heart of who we are—and it comes across more clearly in some communications than others. We see it everywhere, from the way our customers talk about us to the lists we get included on to the thousands of employees who see us as a mission-driven brand; they want to know more about what . . . the mission [is], and they want us to define what the change is that we want in the world."

We ask Laura what she is most proud of in her time at the company, and she says, "When you start out as a start-up you don't have a lot of money to make change with. What we did have was the spirit of our employees who wanted to get out into the community and make a difference. So we really built a culture of giving inside the team. And because we had Jessica, other people wanted us to join in their campaigns. And obviously the products we are making, in everything we do, we're making responsible, healthy, safe products, which makes people feel like they are providing healthy, safe options for their family."

The sheer diversity and number of programs that the Honest Company supports is quite staggering. "We've tried a lot of things; we've been really willing to give to a lot of different programs, and it's only been in the last year that we've asked, 'What's unique that needs a lot of help, that we can really focus on and make a big difference [in]?' First, investing in environmental health research, taking what we've learned and translating that into programs and interventions that can really help in the early education space, and really trying to take some of those program impact results and trying to change policy—so that there really are standards and regulations that make health and safety more accessible to everyone.

"We started to see a lot of people like our products, and a lot of people like our education, so we started to see that we really had a bit of influence. So we started to think about how we would use those assets and those resources to do the most good. And that's when we started to look at investment, and we were starting to see problems in the world that were unsolved. So one of the investments we made was in creating the Honest [Company] Ultra Clean Room at Mt. Sinai Children's Environmental Health Center.

"Before this, scientists were needing to take lab samples for environmental health research and send them out for testing, which could take up to eighteen months. Now with the Ultra Clean Room, where they can do the testing in-house, that turnaround time has been reduced to two weeks. We've already seen some really interesting developments come out of that Clean Room. We're not funding research, but by creating the Clean Room, it attracted amazing researchers, which has started to give us things like methodologies for testing autism in kids under two years old, which didn't exist before. We see things like autism, allergies, early childhood diseases rising, and there are a lot of questions that parents are asking: 'Why is that happening? Is it genetics, is there anything else going on?' And our hope is that we can help find some answers. Does the environment have anything to do with it and, if so, what? How do we gather information so we can make choices? I'm really proud of the work we are doing with the Ultra Clean Room."

Hearing Laura talk with such passion and enthusiasm about her work makes us realize that another fascinating aspect of the story is how backing up "the Promise" with "the Proof" also works in another way. When brands get involved in a cause and use it in their marketing (like, for instance, Dove has done with its "Campaign for Real Beauty"), then if the brand does not put their money where their mouth is [by] actively engaging in partnering with organizations to take action (like Dove has done to partner with entities like the Girl Guides, Girl Scouts, and the Boys & Girls Club to help start programs around self-esteem and body confidence issues), then it is just empty rhetoric. It is exploitation of an issue for brand benefit without contributing anything in return. Customers are too savvy these days to just accept this; in the era of the Internet, it is all too easy to see exactly what companies are doing to back up their claims.

"In the last year, we have also identified another area in which we can make a difference; early education settings are a truly underfunded space. Only 4 percent of public funding goes into early education, but the early years of education, up to age five, are the most important for a child's development. Sixty percent of moms go back to work within six months of giving birth, which means that moms and dads need to rely on child care, and there's no standards for 'What is a healthy, safe place for my kid?' There's a lot of work being done on healthy, safe schools, but child care doesn't have access to information, to healthy, safe nutrition programs, programs on health and safety; they even have requirements on cleaning with bleach! And we'd like to see some standards created on what is a healthy, safe early child-care environment because 12.5 million kids are in a child care center, which is a hugely influential thing for them. And so far, we feel like we've been making a pretty big dent. We've donated a lot of our products to child-care centers, and we've helped over a hundred thousand children so far."

Laure clarifies that she thinks there is still a need to have marketing communication that is focused on products and their attributes.

"Of course, it's a balance between efficacy, which is hugely important because nobody wants to use a product which doesn't work, and the social goodness; and we can dial up different pieces of that depending on what we talk about. But it's important that those values are clear to our customers. I think a lot of go-forward communications to our customers are going to articulate the tangible and easy things . . . that they can do. Our customers have certainly shown that they do want health and safety to be accessible to everyone, and they love that we are a brand focused on creating a movement—that means something to them."

Laura talks about the level of engagement and advocacy from their community and stakeholders. "A portion of every purchase helps fund our programs, so just by purchasing they are helping to make a difference; we message that on every product we sell. We create special opportunities for them to engage with us, whether it is a social media campaign, where if you use a hashtag you can generate funds, which we can use for a particular program. We try to have some activation opportunities for our customers to engage with us, like when we went to Capitol Hill in June to talk about the Toxic Substance Control Act and the reform that's being considered in Congress right now. And rather than put up a petition, we put up a video of Jessica and Christopher and their visit, and we saw huge engagement levels around that—three times the norm.

"If you look at how fast the company has grown, and how fast we got to 1.4 million followers on Facebook, I think we are seeing that people are hungry for these solutions and what we're offering. So I am seeing a really high level of engagement in the purpose of the brand; I want to bring health and safety to my family, and I want to bring it to my community."

This ties into something we have seen everywhere; people are hungry to get involved in something that is meaningful, something that is bigger than themselves. If brands can provide opportunities for participation, we feel that this is something way more powerful than traditional marketing; inside of being selfishly focused on getting the brand's message across, the brand can provide a platform to create a movement built around common cause, providing people with an avenue to participate. To put it another way, it's the customers themselves who can provide the "Proof" to back up the "Promise."

WHY WE LOVE THIS EXAMPLE: The Honest Company has redefined CSR to provide that "Proof" in a living, breathing way. Instead of it being the "window dressing" it all too often is at major companies, a chance to deflect criticism with some well-publicized photo opportunities and charitable donations, at the Honest Company it is something deeply rooted in the purpose of the company. Not only does the Honest Company give a broad range of scalable, flexible opportunities for employees to take ownership across the country, it also goes above and beyond in backing flagship projects like the Ultra Clean Room, all of which help provide multiple sources of "Proof" that the company is serving its purpose of building "healthier, safer families."

Bobby Campbell

Manager, Lady Gaga

Few artists have more successfully leveraged their artistic voice in service of their social voice than Lady Gaga. Her fearlessness in tackling some of the most controversial issues of our time has directly fueled the deep devotion that her fanbase of "Little Monsters" has for her. We talk to her manager, Bobby Campbell, about how she walks that artistic tightrope.

The lights go up at the Dolby Theatre in Hollywood, California. It is the 2016 Academy Awards and the Vice President of the United States, Joe Biden, walks onstage and gives an impassioned speech about the issue of sexual abuse and the need to create a culture of consent. He then introduces Lady Gaga, who performs her Oscar-nominated song "Til It Happens to You" from the documentary film *The Hunting Ground*, which covers the issue of sexual abuse on college campuses. At a pivotal moment she is joined by fifty survivors of sexual abuse, all of whom have written messages like "Not Your Fault" and "Unbreakable" on their arms in support of the performance. When Gaga raises her arm, you can clearly see the word "Survivor" written there too, signaling that she too has been a victim. It is a powerful, raw, vulnerable statement that very few artists in the world could have pulled off except Gaga.

It culminates an extraordinary few months in American history, in which some of the biggest artists in the world have used highly visible pop culture moments to draw attention to social issues. Beyoncé chose the Super Bowl to drop her "Formation" single and highlight the issues around police brutality, Kendrick Lamar's thrilling, visceral performance at the Grammy's proudly supported #BlackLivesMatter, and Gaga's Oscar performance closed out the trifecta (not to mention Leonardo DiCaprio also using his long-awaited Oscar win to highlight the issues around climate change). It's been a long time since major artists were this openly activist about the issues facing America, and it signals a new willingness on their part to use their spotlight to drive social change.

Of course, Stephanie Germanotta aka Lady Gaga has always been using her platform to drive social change, ever since her inception as the fabulous, outrageous Lady Gaga. From the very beginning she has used her art and her music to challenge the status quo and speak up for the voiceless. Whether it's calling for the repeal of "Don't ask, don't tell," fighting for marriage equality, or fearlessly tweeting pictures of herself to draw attention to bulimia and body-image issues, throughout her career Lady Gaga has been as closely identified with her activism as for her art. Perhaps that is what makes her so revered by her army of fans (called Little Monsters), 61 million of them on Facebook and 58 million on Twitter alone, all of whom follow her with a passionate intensity not seen for any other musician of her time.

One of the people who has been by Gaga's side since the beginning is her manager, Bobby Campbell. Slim and animated, he attended the annual SXSW music and tech festival in Austin, Texas, where we caught up with him, fresh off a panel talking about how brands and artists can collaborate to do more good. We sit in the garden of the Four Seasons and talk about his remarkable journey and the work he has done with Gaga to help with both her artistic and social goals.

"So I was part of her journey from the beginning, and I was fortunate to be a part of that," he says. "We put together club tours that she would go play three clubs a night; a pop club, a hip-hop club, and a gay club all over the country. And it was amazing, but for me growing up a young gay kid who didn't come out until I was in college, it wasn't just that I loved the music or the visual; I loved everything about her. I loved her as a person, but there was a deeper meaning for me, in that she is an icon for a generation that I wish I had had, you know? You know, she was out speaking at gay rallies and helping to change what would affect my personal life. How could you want to work with anyone else?"

Bobby talks about some of the challenges that come with artists who want to exercise that social responsibility. "It's interesting a lot of times when you are trying to be a champion for or use your voice for changing things, people don't always want to hear it. Sometimes people just want to be entertained and have fun, and they don't want anything surprising. I believe that she will be around, doing what she does, for the next fifty years. Without a doubt. You look at Tony Bennett and he's an American classic, but if you do the research, in the '60s he was a huge voice in the civil rights movement. And I know in my heart that [Gaga] will be around forever, and will continue to change the world over and over. And like I said before, I think she's only begun to scratch the surface. My personal mission was to get people to understand and respect the person that I know."

Gaga has always used her art to provoke society in service of a deeper message; that's what makes her more interesting than many of the more disposable pop stars in the culture today. And the emotion that she creates because of this courage is something that inspires a level of response that is spontaneous and visceral. "After the Oscars she flew the day after to Chicago, to spend some time off with her fiancé," Bobby says. "And so she's in LAX, and there are grown men, grown women . . . people who would not be what you'd expect to be a Lady Gaga fan, coming up to her in tears, crying, and saying, 'Thank you. Thank you for what you've done.' And they all had some personal story connecting to the conversation on sexual assault and what that meant."

It's the way Gaga can channel grief, be vulnerable, be human. Her music doesn't make the cause great. Her causes make her music great. That's what allows her message to scale outside her gigantic fan base of Little Monsters and reach the mainstream of America. Not that this emotionally courageous approach doesn't take its toll on the artist—or unleash a storm of criticism itself. Bobby talks about some of the challenges that come with the territory.

"When you put your heart into everything you do, it all hurts," he says. "So sometimes part of the challenge is to just keep going. Despite any sort of dissent. Because when you're being a revolutionary or pioneer or actually trying to change the world, you're going to piss people off. You're going to piss people off that are fond of the status quo . . . don't want to rock the boat, right? But being able to just rise above that, to ignore it and say, 'You know what? My purpose here is much greater than maybe this person or this group can understand today. Maybe five years from now or ten years from now or thirty years from now they'll understand it better, but I've got to keep going today. And I've got to fight the fight today. Because if I don't do it, who's going to do it?'"

Bobby talks about some of the decision-making process that happens when Gaga decides to get involved in different causes. He says, "We have to figure out where her voice is strongest. She touches a lot of things—LGBT issues, sexual assault issues—but it still comes from her purpose; her purpose is things she's connected to. If it's something that's great but she doesn't' have a personal connection to the story—not that it doesn't matter to her, right?—there's only so much you can do. I think once an artist does too much, it kind of just dilutes the voice. The thing with sexual assault was, it's something that she really, really, really, really feels strongly about. As someone who had experience with abuse and didn't know what to do with it at the time other than suppress it, now ten years later, she's like, 'OK, I now am in this position. I'm going to make sure what happened to me never happens to any other woman again. Or man. This is not acceptable behavior. And [we] need as a group to discuss this. And to really make people understand that this is not OK.'"

At the core of their philosophy is a simple idea. "Treating people right. You know? Because that just really extends to all of it. If you're treating someone right, something that happened to her in the studio when she was nineteen wouldn't have happened. If you're treating someone right, you're not going to be bullying someone in school. If you're treating someone right, you're not going to have a problem with whom the fuck they want to be. And so that's what we had to boil down when we were putting the Born This Way Foundation together: 'What is the mission of the foundation?' Creating a kinder, braver world . . . that's not a tangible thing. We did this launch event with Oprah at Harvard, and Gaga sat on the stage and she said, 'I am trying to create a behavioral shift. I am trying to change the way people think and interact with one another.' And that's a big, lofty goal."

WHEN YOU'RE BEING A
REVOLUTIONARY OR PIONEER
OR ACTUALLY TRYING TO
CHANGE THE WORLD,
YOU'RE GOING TO
PISS PEOPLE OFF.

BOBBY CAMPBELL

According to the Born This Way Foundation's website, its mission is to "create a safe place to celebrate individuality, to teach advocacy, promote civic engagement, and encourage self-expression, and to provide ways to implement solutions and impact local communities." The foundation has partnered with nonprofit community organizations such as Campus Pride, GLSEN, the National Association of School Psychologists and Youth Service America. Bobby talks about his extremely close working relationship with the foundation. He says, "I work with the Born This Way Foundation team every single day. I help them oversee the connectivity to her, the authenticity to her, working with marketing and partnerships. It's important I stay extremely involved, because it's not a side project; it's part of her overall career."

Bobby talks about a partnership with the National Council for Behavioral Health and Viacom that was a powerful example of providing her fans with resources and help. He says, "When we did the Born This Way tour in 2013, during the US leg, we had a Born Brave bus, which was a pop-up activation from the Born This Way Foundation [that] was an actual bus that we . . . retrofitted with this interactive experience. And a 600-square-foot kind of carnival was there, and there was food and music. We tried to make it a fun tailgate, with live music and food, but then we dug a little deeper. We partnered with local organizations around the country in mental health issues, LGBT issues, body image issues—you name it—to connect youth to organizations already doing great work in their communities.

"But when the bus left at the end of the day, we didn't want to create a gap. So we partnered with local YMCAs or Trevor Project local branches to connect them to the places they might not be aware of or they might not have the courage to go to as yet for whatever reason, and try to foster relationships. And every single organization that was involved was blown away by the amount of people they reached. We had kids . . . there were grandparents bringing their four-year-old transgender grandchild who were coming . . . it was really, really phenomenal."

Bobby highlights how important it was to find partners, in both brands and nonprofits, who had a common purpose to what the artist was trying to achieve. He says, "I think there are times that it's just not for the money, it's about what is the message or the reaction you're trying to achieve. But there are times you have to find the right partner who is willing to say, 'We believe in what you're doing, we want to be part of it, and we're going to help you make it happen financially. Over the course of two months, we engaged with 150,000 young people, in person—not just through social media. It was about creating an experience, and we couldn't have done that on our own. When you talk about providing free food, entertainment, it gets very costly very quick, so we were fortunate to have foundational partners to help fund it, and then Viacom became our media partner and helped to really augment the conversation of what we were doing but also helped find us funding for it."

Another great example is the work Lady Gaga did with Virgin Mobile around her Born This Way Ball tour. Virgin Mobile's RE*-Generation program, which supports helping LGBT and at-risk homeless youth, partnered with the tour to raise funds and awareness. Fans at the shows were encouraged to text to donate money to the cause, with Gaga herself matching funds to $25,000, while fans who had donated eight hours of time to helping at-risk youth were awarded free tickets to the shows. On top of that, during each show, one lucky fan in attendance was called onstage by Gaga and told that Virgin Mobile would give $20,000 to a charity of their choice.

Other brand collaborations for good that Gaga has done include partnering with MAC Cosmetics to launch a line of lipsticks with their Viva Glam line, which has raised more than $202 million to fight HIV and AIDS. And at the time this book went to press, Gaga and Sir Elton John had also teamed up to launch their Love Bravery collection of clothing at Macy's, themed around the idea of inspiring kindness and living courageously. Through that collaboration, 25 percent of the proceeds from each piece will be divided between the Born This Way and Elton John AIDS Foundations.

Bobby talks about how some of their partnerships have come about with conversations with the CSR departments, not just the marketing departments. He brings up a collaboration with Mattel, around their Monster High line of toys, based on the sons and daughters of famous monsters. It is a $1 billion franchise that includes TV specials, video games, merchandise, as well as a movie that is in the works. Gaga will be designing a doll to be launched later in 2016 that will help "inspire empowerment and acceptance among young people."

Bobby says, "The initiative that the Born This Way foundation is doing with Mattel and Monster High, that started at the CSR level. So the Born This Way foundation started a relationship with Bob Goodwin; he runs CSR across Mattel across all of their brands. And there was a courting period: we got to know Bob and the corporate culture at Mattel and what they wanted to do from a philanthropic standpoint, and he got to know what we do at the foundation. And he said, 'OK, Monster High is where we need to work. Monster High is about expressing individuality and celebrating differences,' and six months later we just announced that we're doing a doll with Monster High that Gaga is designing with her sister that will be sold, and the proceeds will benefit the foundation. So I think that meaningful things can happen from either end, and it's just really about getting everyone out at the table and seeing what the commonality is like and how you can build on th[at]."

After stealing the cultural spotlight so conclusively (performing a knockout rendition of the American national anthem at the Super Bowl, winning an Emmy for her acting in *American Horror Story*, the aforementioned Oscar performance, etc.), Gaga and Bobby look ahead to what they want to achieve next in an America that is more divided than ever before.

He says, "I'm fortunate to have grown up in a world where it's not cool to be an asshole. And seeing what's happening now with Trump and all these racists coming out of the woodwork, all over America it's frightening. And it makes me feel so disconnected from my country, in the sense that it's so different from the world that I know and have grown up in my whole life. So I definitely need to ensure that every single day I am giving back by doing some good. It's just kind of part of who I am.

"And it's funny that she and I talk about goals; yeah, it's great to have hit records and sold-out tours and stuff like that, but at the core . . . her interests are so much deeper than that, as are mine. She makes great entertainment, and great performance and great music, and I definitely want to go to her concert . . . but boy does she stand for something else in life. The legacy that will be established over time is so much bigger than how many No. 1s [she'll have] in the hall of records. And you know, that to me is ultimately the mark that she and I want to leave. And it's important; without those things you don't really have the voice to effect the change so they all work together, but to sit and dream about what the world could be like when our kids are growing up, when our grandkids are growing up, that's what gets me really excited."

WHY WE LOVE THIS EXAMPLE: In our journey on this book, we realized many of the most successful artists of any generation are the ones blessed not just with a creative imagination but also a moral imagination—which is the ability to see the world as it should be, not as it is. Whether it is Billie Holiday singing "Strange Fruit" about the horrors of lynching in the Deep South, Harry Belafonte leading the charge on civil rights, or John Lennon and Yoko Ono staging "bed-ins" to protest the Vietnam War, they understand that their art is a means to an end. The work that Bobby is doing with Gaga shows that you can exercise that moral imagination in tandem with a creative one, to have a genuine social impact that can last for generations.

Andy Fyfe

Community Development, B Lab

One of the easiest ways for people to see that the products they purchase are made in an ethical, sustainable way is by certifications—like Fair Trade for coffee, for example. But what if you want to find out about a company, not just a product? B Corps are for-profit companies certified by the nonprofit B Lab to meet rigorous standards of social and environmental performance, accountability, and transparency. They are an assurance that a company isn't just making a "Promise" but is also committing to providing the "Proof."

Our next profile is someone who doesn't just work on one brand but in fact a whole community of brands (more than 1,400), helping them find ways to do well by doing good. Andy Fyfe is the head of community development for B Lab, a nonprofit entity that is behind the B Corps revolution in America. We meet Andy at the modest B Lab office in Tribeca, in downtown New York. Quiet and unassuming, he projects the self-assuredness of someone who has found his purpose in life and is living it every day.

For those of you unfamiliar with what a B Corp is, here's a short primer from Andy. "B Lab, a third-party nonprofit certifies B Corporations the same way Transfair certifies Fair Trade coffee or USGBC certifies green buildings. Certified B Corporations are a new type of corporation [that] uses the power of business to solve social and environmental problems. They work to create greater economic opportunity, strengthen local communities, and preserve our environment. Through a company's B Impact Assessment, anyone can access performance data about the social and environmental practices that stand behind their products. By doing so, good companies can shine brighter and clearer than just good marketing."

Some of the most aspirational and desirable brands in the world are now B Corps. Ben & Jerry's has long been known for its social impact and became a B Corp in 2012. Warby Parker, Etsy, and Patagonia are all B Corps, as is Jessica Alba's start-up the Honest Company, which is now valued at $1.7 billion. *Inc.* magazine called B Corps certification "the highest standard for socially responsible businesses,"[1] while the *New York Times* has said, "B Corp provides what is lacking

---

1 *Inc.* staff. "How a Business Can Change the World." *Inc.* magazine. May 2011. Http://www.inc.com/magazine/20110501/how-a-business-can-change-the-world.html.

elsewhere: proof."[2] In fact, former president Bill Clinton stated, "You ought to look at these B Corporations. . . . We've got to get back to a society that doesn't give one class of stakeholders an inordinate advantage over others."[3]

B Corps are a crucial evolution for a market that is increasingly driven by conscious choices about their consumption. In fact, the importance of "purpose" as a purchase factor has risen 26 percent globally.[4] According to a survey by Cone Communications, "90 percent of Americans say that companies must not only say a product or service is beneficial, but they need to prove it."[5] In 2012, nearly half (47 percent) of customers bought a brand at least monthly that supports a cause, representing a 47 percent increase from 2010.[6] Even a recent study, published by Brookings Institute reported, "Millennials overwhelmingly responded with increased trust (91 percent) and loyalty (89 percent), as well as a stronger likelihood to buy from those companies that supported solutions to specific social issues (89 percent)."[7]

2 Tina Rosenberg, "Ethical Businesses With a Better Bottom Line." *The New York Times.* April 14, 2011. opinionator.blogs.nytimes.com/2011/04/14/ethical-businesses-with-a-better-bottom-line/?_r=0.

3 B Corporation. "President Clinton Talks B Corps." Filmed [July 2012]. YouTube video, 1:58. Posted [August 2012]. https://www.youtube.com/watch?v=2h1T-FaADqR8.

4 Edelman. "Goodpurpose® 2012." 2012.www.edelman.com/insights/intellectual-property/good-purpose/.

5 Cone Communications. "Millenial CSR Study."

6 Edelman. "Goodpurpose® 2012."

7 Morley Winograd and Dr. Michael Hais. "How Millennials Could Upend Wall Street and Corporate America." Governance Studies at Brookings. May 2014. https://www.brookings.edu/wp-content/uploads/2016/06/Brookings_Winogradfinal.pdf

Andy admits an early cynicism on his part about the idea of business as a force for good. He says, "I was very, very skeptical about business in general, really seeking out authenticity and wasn't finding it in a lot of the brands and the way they were communicating it. When I realized there was a community of businesses, brands I have a lot of affinity with, which I wanted to support with my dollar, it was interesting to see that there was a nonprofit working as that backbone, the engine to corral them, verify them, help them scale.

"You see, in University I became skeptical of businesses' efforts to help humanity and our planet. I considered it all greenwashing. I wanted empowerment in their beneficiaries and enlightenment in their affluent consumers. I wanted there to be a way for us as consumers, as business owners, as investors to know exactly the impact a company is having on our environment, society, and its employees. It tied a lot of things together for me. I've been here for five years, and I love it. I always wanted to be a part of something much bigger than myself.

"What I'm seeing is people voting with their dollar for a better pair of eyeglasses, or a pair of shoes, not just with their paycheck, but a much longer investment in voting for where you want to work. And I think that same inclination to see whether my values can be aligned with this purchase is very similar to where you want to spend your day. That's a lot of human capital—what I do from nine to five. When I come to work I don't want to leave my values at home."

When we ask Andy what has changed for him in the five years since he started working for B Lab, his answer is surprising: "I know a lot less now." He elaborates, "The more you know, the less you know. You continue to ask yourself more and more difficult questions. Particularly looking at how B Corps have evolved, we call ourselves B Lab because we are an experiment; we are a laboratory of ideas which have never been put to market. We never really anticipated these things happening as quickly as they did. We're just putting out the recipe and letting the B Corps innovate with what they want to do. The mission is to support a global movement of entrepreneurs using business as a force for good, and using the power of their business to address social and environmental problems. Our ultimate mission is a shared and durable prosperity for all."

What's even more interesting is that it is no longer limited to companies that are manufacturers, with a large carbon footprint. If the twenty-first century is driven by intellectual property and services, then B Corps certification has also evolved to meet these needs.

"Originally when we started, B Corps certification was a way to separate a good company from just good marketing. When you go into Whole Foods or whatever, you're seeing 'organic' or 'fair trade,' which is great, but what about the company behind the product? If you're going to buy that jacket, don't you want to know about the company behind the jacket? Now the B Corps community has evolved to include 121 industries—not just products you buy but services, hospitality, marketing, web design. All these companies are realizing that there is a way to do good and disrupt that industry. More than half the community is made up of service companies; I think that's really relevant."

There are also myriad benefits that come with being part of the B Corps community. "Think about banks; there's a lot of great locally owned CDFI [Community Development Financial Institutions Fund] banks. So through our assessment we ask, 'Who do you bank with?' So it's almost like a business-development opportunity for them to be referred to as a better alternative. A bank is not going to be 'organic' or 'fair trade'; but they are a good bank, and so they deserve to be showcased."

The assessment forces companies not only to look at themselves but at their ecosystem—who they do business with and how ethical they are. Some of the earlier and larger B Corps are now helping their fellow community members not just with advice and consulting in everything from supply chain to marketing but also with financial assistance. For instance, Patagonia has set up the $20 Million & Change fund to invest in companies that are B Corps. Strategic alliances between B Corps are also common; for instance, Method worked with a fellow B Corps called United by Blue, an apparel company that helped collect recycled plastic waste from waterways that Method then used in a line of products. In fact, Seventh Generation goes a step further and actually buys other B Corps as well.

Andy speaks passionately about the need for authenticity in marketing. "More than 50 percent of the workforce is millennials, and more than 50 percent of them want to bring purpose to their work. They see through all of those good marketing campaigns. I was at a conference where Yvon Chouinard, the founder of Patagonia, spoke. The whole room was publicly traded companies talking about their sustainability campaigns, and one of the questions to Yvon was, 'What's your advice for marketing to them and being more authentic?' And he said, 'Stop lying. Everyone here who is under the age of twenty-five, they see through what you're trying to communicate.' I looked around and saw a bunch of young people like me who felt like he was speaking for them; they were just glowing. You can see that shift in generations . . . and to see it spoken by Yvon , who is such a rebel, an accidental businessperson, was amazing."

The B Corps certification now provides an easy shortcut for companies to convey their social-good credentials. "Newer companies who don't have much time to pitch their story can now just use B Corps to encapsulate that impact; it pushes early stage companies to focus not so much on marketing but on their core story. Not many of the B Corps community went to business school or learned marketing, so it is a great shorthand that helps convey the story. Method is an example of a company that is very sleek design, in a very cluttered industry; they don't put the B Corps logo on their product (we don't require it on any brands), but it's baked in the

DNA of their company. It's so much more holistic than CSR or this side-marketing campaign; it's something I really believe in for our company. Which is great because the fresh blood and young energy in the company is saying, 'Huh, maybe we could be a B Corp. Let's give them a call!'

"One of our B Corps, Free Range Studios, [has] this idea around 'making your customer your hero.' Traditional marketing in the past has made you feel like you are the victim or the enemy—'you're not pretty enough' or 'you need to buy this because it will make you better.' Now it's flipping its own on its head, and a lot of B Corps are recognizing that it's that humble approach . . . the brand stops saying it's the hero; we're not solving the world's problems. By their customers being engaged, and them supporting a civil society, they are becoming the hero. That's what really creates that brand allegiance and allows them to be your champion, your best ambassador."

Many Architects of Cool have also gotten involved in the B Corps movement as well. "Woody Harrelson is behind a company called Step Forward paper, which is a certified B Corp, and Jessica Alba, of course, has the Honest Company. We have another B Corp called One World Football, an indestructible, self-inflatable soccer ball. The founder was an incredible inventor who went out and donated soccer balls to communities and came back to find it destroyed—but the kids had designed their own ball from bundled newspaper. It was like 'the power of play'—these kids are already being innovative in their own way. So they designed something which was durable and tapped into that yearning for play, particularly in places like refugee camps. The founder was friends with Sting, who said, 'I believe in this and will fund you.' Long story short, Chevrolet got into the mix and bought 1.8 million soccer balls; and now they have all these ambassadors like Landon Donovan and Brandi Chastain helping to give out these balls."

The kinds of brands that want to be B Corps have also now

changed drastically since the beginning. It's gone from brands designed with purpose at their heart to a lot of major multinational brands like Unilever and Danone thinking about reverse engineering this kind of social commitment into their existence. "When I started we had a few founding B Corps that were larger like Method, but they were primarily small brands. Since then, we've seen Plum Organics being acquired by Campbell's Soup Company, Method being acquired by Ecover, and the Etsy IPO; a lot larger brands have come on board. You have Paul Polman, the CEO of Unilever, saying 'We want to be the largest B Corps.' . . . It could be a challenge for Unilever, but that would never have happened five years ago."

When asked whether he would like to see a world where 100 percent of companies are B Corps, Andy laughs and says, "Yes, absolutely. Our goal is to put ourselves out of work. I think that's going to take a long time. Our goal is to make sure our assessments get more and more rigorous, which will inspire companies to switch things up. Not just for consumers, but for investors, job seekers, academics. . . . Everyone is getting that discerning eye for what's under the hood."

WHY WE LOVE THIS EXAMPLE: At the time this book went to print, there were more than 1,800 companies that had gained B Corp Certification, and more than 4,000 had registered as Benefit Corporations, a statute now legal in more than thirty states. Andy and the team at B Lab are showing that in just a short period of time, an enormous amount of change can take place. They are showing that giving people a chance to identify ethical companies has exponential dividends in helping accelerate the growth of businesses that have a social impact—as well as holding those companies to backing up their word with their deeds. B Corps are the vanguard of a new type of capitalism, a ray of hope showing that business leaders are open to a new model.

PART III

HOW TO GET STARTED TODAY

STEPS TO GET STARTED

1 FIND YOUR (INTERNAL) ALLIES

2 START WITH WHAT YOU HAVE

3 CLARITY FOLLOWS ACTIONS

8 SHARE YOUR WORK

9 PAY IT FORWARD

4 DON'T FEAR ACCUSATIONS OF BRANDWASHING

7 ADD SOME GOOD TO THE BRIEF

6 PRACTICE THE GOLDEN RULE

5 RESPECT THE PROPORTIONS

DREAM IT, DO IT, SHARE IT!

OK. You've read all of these inspiring stories of people and their paths to purpose. Now it's your turn.

As authors, our goal is to inspire you and others to join in this movement and be better marketers and citizens by balancing profit and the needs of your customers and communities while still innovating and harnessing the force of popular culture.

It may seem daunting; it may seem like an impossible mountain to climb. But here are some small steps to get you started.

1. Find your (internal) allies: Somewhere inside your organization there is someone else who wants to use their talents and resources to do more good in the world, the same as you. Perhaps it's the veteran CSR person. Perhaps it's the new intern. Whoever they are, seek them out. Put forth your intention to help out into the universe, and you will be amazed by what comes back.

2. Start with what you have: Don't get hung up on the fact you may not have a big budget. Find a way to experiment. Start by donating products or services to an organization you identify with. Do some pro bono work to help meet new people and get out of your comfort zone. Sometimes it takes a while to figure out what inspires you. Get your feet wet and try out a variety of things to see what you identify with the most. Do a "beta test" with a tiny amount of money.

3. Clarity follows action: This is an important one. When you start, you may have no clear idea of how to best make an impact. Sometimes it takes a few tries to figure it out. The important thing is not to be paralyzed by fear. Learning is an iterative process that happens by doing. At the very least, you'll meet some nice folks along the way.

4. Don't fear accusations of brandwashing: Look, all
organizations have something they can be criticized about. Critics
can find ways to attack your business practices, your carbon footprint, a million different things. But that shouldn't paralyze you
into inaction. It shouldn't make you feel cynical about your ability
to create change. Be open and honest about your intentions, and
transparent about how this small action is not intended to solve all
the problems at once. And you will find that amongst the haters,
you will also find allies in what you believe in. After all, the journey
of a thousand miles begins with a single step.

5. Respect the proportions: One of the greatest pieces of ad-
vice we got was from a young entrepreneur who said, "When a brand
spends $10,000 on doing some good, and then $10 million trum-
peting that in an ad campaign, then something smells fishy." That's
when criticisms of brandwashing are accurate, when the proportion
of actual good to amplification of the message is off.

6. Practice the golden rule: Only do things that you would
want to have done to you. Think about what you would like to be on
the receiving end of. Follow your intuition; if something feels wrong
to you, speak up.

7. Add some good to the brief: For professional market-
ers, designers, and creatives, the brief is the most essential part of
the creative process. So vital that brand and design firm Bassett &
Partners produced an entire documentary titled *Briefly* dedicated
to informing and inspiring collaborators to write better briefs to
lead to exceptional creative results. In the film, John Boiler, CEO
of 72andSunny, went as far as to declare: "The role of the creative
brief, I don't think has ever been as important as it is now. It is an

open statement of ambition for a brand or client." So imagine the potential power of impacting a greater good becoming a core part of every brief and brand ambition. That change can help to unleash purpose-driven creativity in profound ways. As Frank Gehry said, "I don't think there is any lack of places to go creatively that wouldn't be worth exploring in the interest of humanity being better."

8. Share your work: For those of you working on interesting projects that aspire to grow sales through making a positive impact in the lives of others in cool ways, go online and post what you are working on with the hashtags #goodisthenewcool and #showyourwork. Austin Kleon, in his best seller *Show Your Work!*, speaks to the importance of sharing your work with communities of like-minded people. We are all drawing inspiration from the endeavors of others on a daily basis, so inspire us all by sharing your works-in-progress, big or small.

9. Pay it forward: Share this book with someone who could benefit from it. We wrote the book we wanted to read—something that spoke to the realities of marketers struggling to find meaning in their work. We want to help other marketers who have a desire to do more than just make people buy more stuff, and we know there are many of us out there. If you know any, please share our stories.

OUR FINAL THOUGHT: THINK TRANSFOR- MATIONAL, NOT TRANSAC- TIONAL

Hopefully all of these stories have inspired you as much as they have inspired us. We feel like we are only at the beginning of a better paradigm, one where courage replaces conformity, empathy replaces apathy, and hope replaces cynicism.

Cynicism, in particular, is what we would like these stories to help you battle—the weariness from hearing all of the negative narratives out there every day—meaningless political friction, corruption and greed. Too often it feels safer to take refuge in a cocoon of meaningless trivia—the latest celebrity scandal, the divisive rhetoric of modern politics—and use that as fuel to believe that this world is past saving. We hope that in some small way, the stories of these inspiring people will help show that there is a better way of doing things. "Good" can keep being "Cool," but only if enough of us commit our time, energy, and passion to helping make this happen.

It starts with all of us understanding a deeper sense of our own purpose, and ensuring we spend our time and talents working for organizations that have a higher order reason for existence other than solely for profit. Through a combination of this self-analysis and dialogue with other stakeholders, we can then find "Allies" who have common cause. It requires all of us to think of people as "Citizens not Consumers," and identify the opportunities that exist for us to not just advertise, but actually "Solve Problems," from the everyday to the epic. We realize that "People Are the New Media" and adding real value to their lives is the best way to turn them into your biggest advocates. We must ensure that when we design our ideas and products, that we "Lead with the Cool and Bake In the Good"—and make sure we always "Back Up the Promise with the Proof." That's how we can ensure that we all help to "Optimize Life" for everyone on this planet.

Beyond those we profiled in this book, there are many more in this growing movement, who are successfully doing this and leading by example. People like superstar Golden State Warriors basketball player Steph Curry, who personally donates mosquito nets to families in Africa via his foundation, Nothing but Nets, every time he scores a three-pointer. Others like Lauren Bush—niece of President George W. Bush—and her fashion start-up, Feed, show that the idea of doing good through cool is nonpartisan. The inspiring millennial entrepreneurs behind Sword & Plough who make beautiful bags and clothes that help fund programs for military veterans; the wonderful jewelry start-up Maiyet that takes the work of artisans from around the world and shows them for the true luxury that they are; the dedicated folks at ReFoundry who help former convicts learn new skills like carpentry that help them create furniture, and so many more. Every day we see new stories that bring us hope and inspiration for what the world can be if we choose to create it.

Certainly, that choice to use our moral imaginations to solve problems will be more important than ever. In the next twenty years, the human population will swell from seven billion to eight billion people: the fastest population growth in the history of the planet. With this growth comes a choice: Do we continue to think in a "transactional" manner about the way our societies operate, continuing to do business as usual and ignoring the larger issues of inequality, discrimination, the environment, and other existential problems? Or do we choose to think in a "transformational" manner, finding new models and solutions to help ensure a fair and prosperous future for all?

To us, the answer couldn't be clearer; whether we work as business leaders, culture creators, or social entrepreneurs, we need to find new ways of working together that rejects the outdated models of the past. We need to find new ways to utilize our unique talents in ways that haven't been possible until now because of the generational, technological, and spiritual awakenings that are affecting us on a profound level.

Now it's up to you.

How will you start today?

RESOURCES AND OTHER LINKS

When writing this book, one of our biggest problems was figuring out which brands to include—there were more examples than we had room for! So we decided to capture all the stories we found inspiring at our blog at www.goodisthenewcool.org. You can find stories, links, and a whole lot more resources there. We hope you'll visit us and say hi.

Further Recommended Reading:

Delivering Happiness by Tony Hsieh
The Story of Purpose by Joey Reiman
Making Good by Billy Parish and Dev Aujla
Social Innovation, Inc. by Jason Saul
The Conscience Economy by Steven Overman
True Story by Ty Montague
Locavesting by Amy Cortese
Enchantment by Guy Kawasaki
Steal Like an Artist by Austin Kleon
Contagious by Jonah Berger
Youtility by Jay Baer
The B Corp Handbook: How to Use Business as a Force for Good by Ryan Honeyman
Let My People Go Surfing by Yvon Chouinard, founder of Patagonia
Breakthrough Nonprofit Branding by Carol Cone

Acknowledgments

Afdhel and Bobby would like to thank agent extraordinaire Robert Guinsler, as well as the amazing team at Regan Arts: Judith, Richard, Brian, Lucas, Emily, Kathryn, Gregory, Clarke, Nancy and everyone else who made this book possible.

Afdhel:

First and foremost I'd like to thank my amazing wife Rukshana for her patience and support while writing the book. I couldn't have done this without you. Thank you also to my parents, friends and family around the world who keep me grounded and loved.

Thanks also to so many people along the way who gave freely of their wisdom, introductions, and support: Jerri Chou, Paul Woolmington, Catrin Thomas, Jules Ferree, Stephanie Kahan, Carol Cone, Joao Rozario, Jack Shea, Jeffrey Moran, Pierre Berard and everyone at Pernod Ricard, Andrew Hampp, Chris Johns, John Moore, Jeff Benjamin, Courtney Ettus, Drew Ianni, Jack Horner, Kiel Berry, Yusra Eliyas, Rikaza Izadeen, Ryan Gill, Sascha Lewis, Jesse Kirshbaum, Lori Corpuz, Rah Crawford, Dinesha Mendis, Robyn Shapiro, Ian Utile, Shiromi Pinto, Anthony Demby, and Tru Pettigrew.

Bobby:

First of all, thank you Renee. I could not have done this without your love and partnership in this amazing journey. I could have written another book thanking all of the people who have touched my life and made this possible; especially my amazing family. There is no way I could thank everyone, but if you are in my life, you are appreciated.

There are some that I want to thank simply for being an inspiration to me along the way:

Miles; Mom and Dad; Lisa; Dickie and Jan; Christian Wright; Kamryn; Jaden; My Direct Impulse, Access and YARDstyle Families; Tony and Kenny Mac; Tru; Dre; Jodi; Eric Dawson; Peace First; Bobbi MacKenzie: Mr. Kilgallon; Ann Christiano; Dao and Maxwell; Ant Demby; Troy; Shelby; Emma Holbrook; Gene; Kea; Kirk; Mike Tucker; Mike Riley; Bev; Ali; The GoodFellas.

About the Authors

Afdhel Aziz and Bobby Jones are two highly experienced marketers, based in New York City. Their friendship and common passion for the idea of "giving back" led them to collaborate on this book, which they hope will inspire other marketers.

BOBBY JONES is one of the nation's most respected experts in marketing to teen and millennial audiences. As an entrepreneur, strategist, and active participant in their world, Bobby has traveled the globe engaging young people and translating those insights into innovative campaigns and strategies for leading global brands such as Adidas, Brand Jordan, Coca-Cola, Heineken, and MTV. Bobby is currently Chief Marketing and Communications Officer (CMCO) of Peace First, where he leads all of its marketing and communications efforts to help young people in over 90 countries around the world to be powerful peacemakers, creating compassionate solutions to the world's injustices. Prior to Peace First, Bobby was Vice President at Octagon North America, where he led the Octagon Access group, the nation's preeminent team for global brands looking to effectively leverage sports, music, and entertainment to reach millennial and multicultural consumers. A proud Washington, D.C. native, Bobby lives in Brooklyn, NY with his wife and young son.

AFDHEL AZIZ is a marketing consultant, coach, and speaker who has worked for blue-chip companies such as Absolut, Nokia, Heineken, and Procter & Gamble. Visionary, inspiring, and fearless, he is an expert on how to deliver cutting-edge campaigns, content, and experiences that drive pop culture, working with a wide range of artists and cultural partners such as Lady Gaga, Deadmau5, the TED Conferences, and the Andy Warhol Foundation. He has been a featured speaker at the Cannes Lions, SXSW, Adweek, and TEDx-Bushwick, and his award-winning work has been featured in the *New York Times*, *Vice*, *Fast Company*, *Forbes*, *Fortune*, the *Guardian*, *Hypebeast*, and others. You can find out more at www.afdhelaziz.com or follow him on Twitter @afdhelaziz.